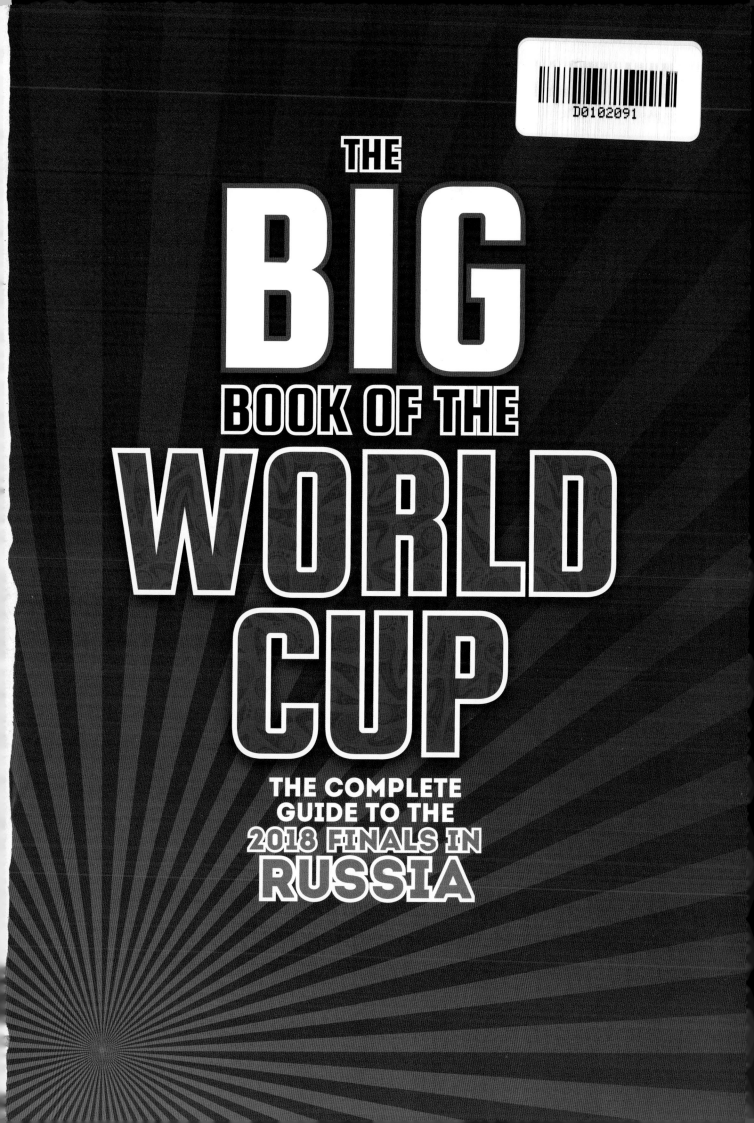

THE
BIG
BOOK OF THE
WORLD
CUP

THE COMPLETE GUIDE TO THE 2018 FINALS IN RUSSIA

Published by Vision Sports Publishing in 2018

Vision Sports Publishing
19-23 High Street
Kingston upon Thames
Surrey
KT1 1LL

www.visionsp.co.uk

ISBN: 978-1909534-83-4

Editors: Jim Drewett and Ed Davis
Authors: Clive Batty and Iain Spragg
Design: Neal Cobourne
Kit images: David Moor, www.historicalkits.co.uk
All pictures: Getty Images

Printed and bound in China by Toppan Leefung PTE Ltd

MIX
Paper from
responsible sources
FSC
www.fsc.org   FSC™ C104723

A CIP record for this book is available from the British Library

All international statistics are correct in *The Big Book of the World Cup 2018* up
until 1 Jan 2018

CONTENTS

FROM RUSSIA WITH LOVE

Russia faced fierce competition for the honour of hosting the 2018 World Cup but eventually emerged victorious thanks to its ambitious plans for a spectacular global festival of football.

There is nothing quite like a World Cup on the horizon to generate excitement and a sense of anticipation. The finals capture the imagination on a truly global scale and billions from every part of the planet will be watching as the drama unfolds in what is shaping up to be another epic tournament.

Russia has reportedly spent approximately £10 billion in readiness to host the finals for the first time. It's a huge investment but represents money well spent for a football-mad nation that cannot wait to welcome the world and showcase the country's history, incredible architecture and outstanding natural beauty.

An array of gleaming new stadia provide the centrepiece of Russia's preparations, and with 2.5 million tickets available for the 64 matches supporters can expect state-of-the-art facilities and a stage worthy of sport's biggest and most vibrant party.

Every host nation brings a unique flavour to the finals and Russia's World Cup promises to be one all about passion and pride as a country of 144 million people builds on the legacy created after it staged the 2014 Winter Olympics.

"Russia loves football," said President Vladimir Putin after the news was confirmed his country had been chosen. "Russia knows what football is and in our country we have everything to conduct the World Cup on a very worthy level."

The 2018 tournament is the 21st edition of the World Cup, and as ever when the beautiful game's finest teams come together every four years the burning question is who will eventually lift the coveted trophy? Only eight nations have ever done so, but given we have a debutant host country could we perhaps also encounter a first-time winner?

Spain triumphed in South Africa in 2010 to become the latest new addition to the list of World Cup-winning nations, and if anyone is going to make history in Russia it's perhaps most likely to be their neighbours across the Iberian border, Portugal, the reigning European champions and Spain's Group B rivals.

It is hard, however, to look much beyond Germany (four-time World Cup winners and the defending champions) and Brazil (the most successful nation in World Cup history with five wins) for our champions. Both sides are in fine fettle going into the tournament and with the assembled talents of Neymar and Toni Kroos, Philippe Coutinho and Mesut Ozil in their ranks, both have the firepower to reign supreme. That said, France, Spain, Argentina and Belgium will also be fancying their chances of glory.

England's expectations are more modest. The Three Lions haven't reached the quarter-finals of the World Cup since they were in the last eight of the 2006 finals in Germany, and after the humiliation in Brazil four years ago the 1966 champions will perhaps simply be relieved to get out of their group this time.

The football gods were in a generous mood when they decided to place Gareth Southgate's side in Group G with Panama and Tunisia, and although Belgium will be England's Everest the chances of respectability and a place in the Round of 16 appear promising.

Elsewhere, the perennial debate whether a team from Central America, Asia or Africa can break Europe and South America's World Cup monopoly will rage on. Tunisia, Costa Rica and Senegal were the highest ranked countries from outside the two dominant footballing continents at the time of the draw and, having reached the quarter-finals in 2002 and cruised through qualification this time around, the Senegalese look the best equipped to mount a challenge in Russia.

Whoever lifts the trophy in Moscow on 15 July will of course be worthy champions. You don't win the World Cup by accident, and all the assembled teams will be dreaming of writing their name into history.

All you have to do is sit back and enjoy a 32-days-long feast of fabulous football.

Russia may not win the tournament, but their fans know how to make themselves heard!

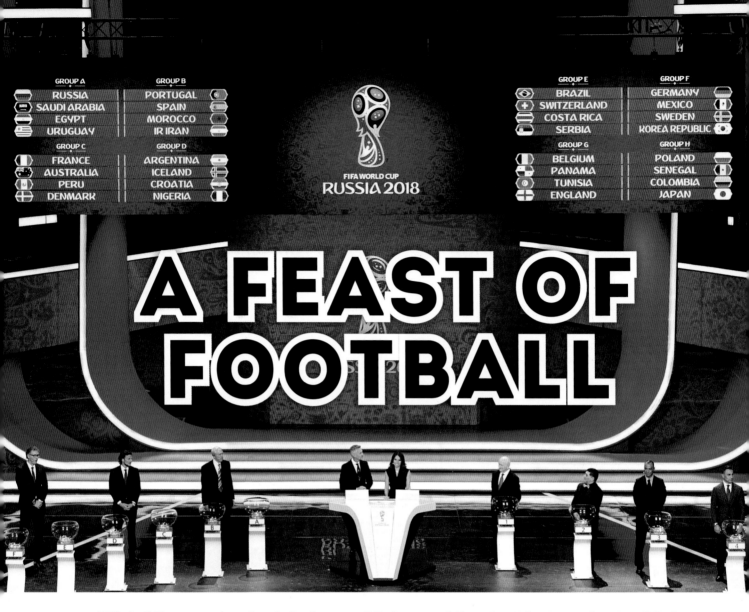

GROUP A	GROUP B
RUSSIA	PORTUGAL
SAUDI ARABIA	SPAIN
EGYPT	MOROCCO
URUGUAY	IR IRAN

GROUP C	GROUP D
FRANCE	ARGENTINA
AUSTRALIA	ICELAND
PERU	CROATIA
DENMARK	NIGERIA

GROUP E	GROUP F
BRAZIL	GERMANY
SWITZERLAND	MEXICO
COSTA RICA	SWEDEN
SERBIA	KOREA REPUBLIC

GROUP G	GROUP H
BELGIUM	POLAND
PANAMA	SENEGAL
TUNISIA	COLOMBIA
ENGLAND	JAPAN

FIFA WORLD CUP
RUSSIA 2018

A FEAST OF FOOTBALL

With 64 games scheduled over 32 days of football in Russia the 2018 World Cup will be the biggest television event of the year as billions across the globe tune in to watch the action.

The reach of the World Cup is truly staggering. The 2014 tournament in Brazil was beamed to 3.2 billion viewers – 44.5 million of them in the UK alone – and there was a total of 98,087 hours of football shown by broadcasters. The competition is made for television.

Even more fans are expected to watch the tournament from the comfort of their armchairs in 2018, and football supporters not making the long journey to Russia will be able to see every minute of every game this summer on their TV.

For the 14th consecutive time, the BBC and ITV are sharing the coverage of the finals and it all kicks off with the eagerly anticipated tournament opener between hosts Russia and Saudi Arabia in Moscow on ITV on 14 June at 4pm UK time. The BBC are in action the following day, a day which features the big Iberian derby in Group B between Spain and Portugal.

The good news for British viewers is that, although the World Cup is being played in four different time zones in Russia, 50 of the 64 fixtures are on Moscow Time just two hours ahead of the UK – there are no late night or early morning fixtures to worry about.

The Three Lions' first group game against Tunisia in Volgograd on 18 June is a 7pm kick-off, while the Panama game in Nizhny Novgorod six days later is a 1pm start. Both are on the BBC, while the mouth-watering third fixture against Belgium in Kaliningrad on 28 June will be shown on ITV at 7pm.

If Gareth Southgate's boys get through to the Round of 16 the BBC will provide the live coverage of the match, and if the side get through to the quarter-finals the BBC has the rights to the potential match on 6 July, while ITV has the rights to the alternative fixture on Saturday 7 July.

WORLD CUP VIEWING GUIDE

All kick-offs are in British Summer Time.

GROUP STAGE

THURSDAY 14 JUNE

4pm – **Russia v Saudi Arabia**, Luzhniki Stadium,
  Moscow (Group A), **ITV**

FRIDAY 15 JUNE

1pm – **Egypt v Uruguay**, Ekaterinburg Arena,
  Yekaterinburg (Group A), **BBC**

4pm – **Morocco v Iran**, Saint Petersburg Stadium,
  Saint Petersburg (Group B), **ITV**

7pm – **Portugal v Spain**, Fisht Stadium,
  Sochi (Group B), **BBC**

SATURDAY 16 JUNE

11am – **France v Australia**, Kazan Arena,
  Kazan (Group C), **BBC**

2pm – **Argentina v Iceland**, Spartak Stadium,
  Moscow (Group D), **ITV**

5pm – **Peru v Denmark**, Mordovia Arena,
  Saransk (Group C), **BBC**

8pm – **Croatia v Nigeria**, Kaliningrad Stadium,
  Kaliningrad (Group D), **ITV**

SUNDAY 17 JUNE

1pm – **Costa Rica v Serbia**, Samara Arena,
  Samara (Group E), **ITV**

4pm – **Germany v Mexico**, Luzhniki Stadium,
  Moscow (Group F), **BBC**

7pm – **Brazil v Switzerland**, Rostov Arena,
  Rostov-on-Don (Group E), **ITV**

MONDAY 18 JUNE

1pm – **Sweden v South Korea**, Nizhny Novgorod
  Stadium, Nizhny Novgorod (Group F), **ITV**

4pm – **Belgium v Panama**, Fisht Stadium, Sochi
  (Group G), **BBC**

7pm – **Tunisia v England**, Volgograd Arena,
  Volgograd (Group G), **BBC**

TUESDAY 19 JUNE

1pm – **Colombia v Japan**, Mordovia Arena,
  Saransk (Group H), **BBC**

4pm – **Poland v Senegal**, Spartak Stadium,
  Moscow (Group H), **ITV**

7pm – **Russia v Egypt**, Saint Petersburg Stadium,
  Saint Petersburg (Group A), **BBC**

Cristiano Ronaldo's Portugal face arch rivals Spain on the opening day of the tournament

WEDNESDAY 20 JUNE

1pm – **Portugal v Morocco**, Luzhniki Stadium,
  Moscow (Group B), **BBC**

4pm – **Uruguay v Saudi Arabia**, Rostov Arena,
  Rostov-on-Don (Group A), **BBC**

7pm – **Iran v Spain**, Kazan Arena, Kazan (Group B), **ITV**

THURSDAY 21 JUNE

1pm – **Denmark v Australia**, Samara Arena, Samara (Group C), **ITV**

4pm – **France v Peru**, Ekaterinburg Arena, Yekaterinburg (Group C), **ITV**

7pm – **Argentina v Croatia**, Nizhny Novgorod Stadium, Nizhny Novgorod (Group D), **BBC**

FRIDAY 22 JUNE

1pm – **Brazil v Costa Rica**, Saint Petersburg Stadium, Saint Petersburg (Group E), **ITV**

4pm – **Nigeria v Iceland**, Volgograd Arena, Volgograd (Group D), **BBC**

7pm – **Serbia v Switzerland**, Kaliningrad Stadium, Kaliningrad (Group E), **BBC**

SATURDAY 23 JUNE

1pm – **Belgium v Tunisia**, Spartak Stadium, Moscow (Group G), **BBC**

4pm – **South Korea v Mexico**, Rostov Arena, Rostov-on-Don (Group F), **ITV**

7pm – **Germany v Sweden**, Fisht Stadium, Sochi (Group F), **ITV**

SUNDAY 24 JUNE

1pm – **England v Panama**, Nizhny Novgorod Stadium, Nizhny Novgorod (Group G), **BBC**

4pm – **Japan v Senegal**, Ekaterinburg Arena, Yekaterinburg (Group H), **BBC**

7pm – **Poland v Colombia**, Kazan Arena, Kazan (Group H), **ITV**

MONDAY 25 JUNE

3pm – **Uruguay v Russia**, Samara Arena, Samara (Group A), **ITV**

3pm – **Saudi Arabia v Egypt**, Volgograd Arena, Volgograd (Group A), **ITV4**

7pm – **Iran v Portugal**, Mordovia Arena, Saransk (Group B), **BBC**

7pm – **Spain v Morocco**, Kaliningrad Stadium, Kaliningrad (Group B), **BBC**

TUESDAY 26 JUNE

3pm – **Denmark v France**, Luzhniki Stadium, Moscow (Group C), **ITV**

3pm – **Australia v Peru**, Fisht Stadium, Sochi (Group C), **ITV4**

7pm – **Nigeria v Argentina**, Saint Petersburg Stadium, Saint Petersburg (Group D), **BBC**

7pm – **Iceland v Croatia**, Rostov Arena, Rostov-on-Don (Group D), **BBC**

WEDNESDAY 27 JUNE

3pm – **Mexico v Sweden**, Ekaterinburg Arena, Yekaterinburg (Group F), **BBC**

3pm – **South Korea v Germany**, Kazan Arena, Kazan (Group F), **BBC**

7pm – **Serbia v Brazil**, Spartak Stadium, Moscow (Group E), **ITV**

7pm – **Switzerland v Costa Rica**, Nizhny Novgorod Stadium, Nizhny Novgorod (Group E), **ITV4**

THURSDAY 28 JUNE

3pm – **Japan v Poland**, Volgograd Arena, Volgograd (Group H), **BBC**

England take on Eden Hazard's Belgium in the crunch Group G match on 28 June

3pm – **Senegal v Colombia**, Samara Arena, Samara (Group H), **BBC**

7pm – **Panama v Tunisia**, Mordovia Arena, Saransk (Group G), **ITV4**

7pm – **England v Belgium**, Kaliningrad Stadium, Kaliningrad (Group G), **ITV**

ROUND OF 16

SATURDAY 30 JUNE

1: 3pm – **Winner Group C v Runner-up Group D**, Kazan Arena, Kazan, **ITV**

2: 7pm – **Winner Group A v Runner-up Group B**, Fisht Stadium, Sochi, **ITV**

SUNDAY 1 JULY

3: 3pm – **Winner Group B v Runner-up Group A**, Luzhniki Stadium, Moscow, **BBC**

4: 7pm – **Winner Group D v Runner-up Group C**, Nizhny Novgorod Stadium, Nizhny Novgorod, **ITV**

MONDAY 2 JULY

5: 3pm – **Winner Group E v Runner-up Group F**, Samara Arena, Samara, **BBC**

6: 7pm – **Winner Group G v Runner-up Group H**, Rostov Arena, Rostov-on-Don, **BBC**

TUESDAY 3 JULY

7: 3pm – **Winner Group F v Runner-up Group E**, Saint Petersburg Stadium, Saint Petersburg, **ITV**

8: 7pm – **Winner Group H v Runner-up Group G**, Spartak Stadium, Moscow, **BBC**

QUARTER-FINALS

FRIDAY 6 JULY

QF 1: 3pm – **Winner Match 1 v Winner Match 2**, Nizhny Novgorod Stadium, **BBC**

QF 2: 7pm – **Winner Match 5 v Winner Match 6**, Kazan Arena, Kazan, **BBC**

SATURDAY 7 JULY

QF 3: 1pm – **Winner Match 7 v Winner Match 8**, Samara Arena, Samara, **ITV**

QF 4: 7pm – **Winner Match 3 v Winner Match 4**, Fisht Stadium, Sochi, **ITV**

SEMI-FINALS

TUESDAY 10 JULY

SF 1: 7pm – **Winner QF 1 v Winner QF 2**, Saint Petersburg Stadium, Saint Petersburg, **ITV**

WEDNESDAY 11 JULY

SF 2: 7pm – **Winner QF 3 v Winner QF 4**, Luzhniki Stadium, Moscow, **BBC**

THIRD PLACE PLAY-OFF

SATURDAY 14 JULY

3pm – **Loser SF 1 v Loser SF 2**, Saint Petersburg Stadium, Saint Petersburg, **ITV**

FINAL

SUNDAY 15 JULY

4pm – **Winner SF1 v Winner SF 2**, Luzhniki Stadium, Moscow, **BBC & ITV**

Will Brazil be celebrating after the final on 15 July?

THE HOSTS WITH THE MOST

Sixty years after first welcoming the former Soviet Union to the party, the World Cup heads to Russia for an exciting new chapter in the story of football's greatest global gathering.

The World Cup has always been a tournament conducted on the grandest of scales. The finals are the most spectacular show in sport and when the beautiful game and its finest teams descend on Russia in 2018 for the first time the World Cup will be played out on the biggest stage of them all.

Everything about Russia is big. Measuring in at a staggering 6.6 million square miles, it's the largest country by area on the planet. One eighth of the world's inhabited land mass is Russian and its 144 million people, speaking more than 100 languages,

make it the ninth most populous. It covers 11 of Earth's 24 different time zones and even though the World Cup will be staged in the western half of the country to make the tournament more manageable in terms of journey times, some of the distances between the venues are still truly staggering.

The trip, for example, from the port city of Saint Petersburg on the Baltic Sea in the north to Sochi on the Black Sea in the south is 1,200 miles. The distance between Kaliningrad in the extreme west to Yekaterinburg in the east is even longer at 1,540 miles.

The country is – by any geographical, political or sporting measure – a global giant and it is no surprise then that Fifa has finally chosen the world's biggest nation to host the game's greatest event.

"Our country is looking forward to the World Cup and it is going to hold a top-notch event to let the leading footballers display their skills and show what real football is all about," said Russian President Vladimir Putin. "We'll make everything possible so that the tournament will become a true sports holiday and, what is most important, bring closer together the big and friendly football family, the family that values sports, friendship and fair contest.

"Fans will feel our traditional hospitality and openness, the more so as the World Cup matches will be played in 11 Russian cities and fans will have a

A stunning aerial view of the magnificent Luzhniki Stadium in Moscow

chance to visit several regions of our country, which is so enormous and diverse. And anyone who has been in Russia at least once knows how hospitable we are to our friends."

Russia had bid for the honour of hosting the finals only once before. That was in 1990 when it was still the Soviet Union but the Communist state lost out to Italy and it was not until 2009, when Fifa invited countries to express an interest in staging the 2018 tournament, that Russia decided to step forward again.

Football's governing body convened in Zurich in December 2010 to announce the winner. Despite a close call in the first round of voting, Russia fended off

Russia is hosting the finals for the first time and will be determined to put on a spectacular show

the rival joint bid of Spain and Portugal in the second round to be confirmed as the 16th different nation to welcome the World Cup.

The news that Russia had won also meant they were the third first-time hosts in the last five tournaments, and as was the case in Japan and South Korea in 2002 and South Africa eight years later the country was quickly gripped by a sense of national anticipation.

The Russian authorities have matched that mood with the hard cash that is inevitably required to make such an enormous event a reality. An estimated £10 billion has been spent on the tournament, half of which has come directly from the Russian government, and the gleaming new stadia which have been built as a result of the investment are evidence of a country ready to make its mark. The Saint Petersburg Stadium is the second largest of the new grounds, but at a cost of £615 million to construct it will be the most expensive on show.

Russia has also dug deep to improve its infrastructure ahead of the finals. Volgograd Airport has a new international terminal to accommodate the arrival of supporters. Samara's Kurumoch International Airport has also undergone major rebuilding, while the country's electricity, IT and communications infrastructure have all been upgraded. More than 100 new hotels have been built in eight of the host cities to provide accommodation for visiting fans over the month-long duration of the competition.

The initial demand for tickets for the finals has more than justified Russia's spending. A grand total of 2.5 million will ultimately be made available by the organising committee for the 64 matches, and by November 2017 Fifa confirmed they had sold 742,760 tickets in the first round of sales.

Some 53 per cent of applications were made by Russian fans but a reflection of the truly international nature of the 2018 World Cup was the 47 per cent – nearly 350,000 – submissions made by supporters from further afield. Fans from the United States, Brazil, Germany, China, Mexico, Israel, Argentina, Australia, and England were the most eager to attend the finals among the non-Russian allocation.

"We are very pleased with the results of the first sales phase," Fifa's head of ticketing Falk Eller said. "They confirmed the great interest sparked by the World Cup in Russia – both at local and international level."

Innovation has always been part of the World Cup's DNA and 2018 will be no different with the introduction of a FAN ID for all those travelling to the tournament. The ID has been introduced in place of the visa normally required to enter Russia, streamlining the process but more importantly from the supporters' perspective it will give them access to free public transport. That includes inter-city trains for those long journeys that are part and parcel of following a competition in such a vast country.

Russia's love affair with the beautiful game began in the early 20th century before the dawn of the Soviet era. The rise of Communism in 1918, however, did

the country had well and truly caught the World Cup bug and the next three finals saw the Soviet Union make significant strides forward.

Another quarter-final appearance in Chile in 1962 was further proof the

nothing to diminish the appetite for the sport but the country's relationship with the World Cup was initially an uneasy one. The Soviet Union declined to enter the first five tournaments and it was not until 1958 that a team was belatedly dispatched to compete in Sweden.

It was the start of a golden era for Soviet football. The side battled through to the quarter-finals in 1958, going down to their Swedish hosts in the last eight, but

side were a force to be reckoned with. It could have been even better for Gavriil Kachalin's team, but once again they faced the host nation in the last eight and they bowed out of the tournament following a 2-1 defeat in the city of Arica.

The 1966 finals in England, however, were a different story. The Soviets famously beat the two-time world champions Italy in the group stages and then, at the

Zabivaka, the official mascot for the 2018 finals

The absolutely stunning Saint Petersburg Stadium will play host to seven matches during the tournament

Russia's famous cossack-style dance could well become the tournament's favourite goal celebration

third time of asking, progressed beyond the quarter-finals after beating Hungary 2-1 in Sunderland. The mighty West Germans were their opponents in the last four, and although the game at Goodison Park ended in a 2-1 defeat the team returned home with their heads held high and the worldwide reputation of Soviet football significantly enhanced.

Four years later the Soviets headed to Mexico for their fourth consecutive World Cup appearance. A crushing 4-1 victory over Belgium and a goalless draw with the hosts in the group stages ensured the side once again made it through to the knockout phase, but the adventure was brought to a heartbreaking end by Uruguay who scored a 117th-minute extra-time winner in the quarter-final in the famous Azteca Stadium in Mexico City.

Politics sadly meant there was no Soviet Union side in West Germany in 1974. The politburo refused the team permission to play Chile in a play-off match because of the leadership of the South American country's anti-Communist stance and when the side failed to qualify on merit four years later, the good times were effectively over.

They were back at the top table in Spain in 1982, in Mexico four years later and Italy in 1990 but the old magic eluded them and the collapse of the USSR a year later brought to an end the story of the Soviet side at the finals of the World Cup.

Russia's first solo World Cup foray was not long in the making as the team successfully qualified for USA '94. Brazil and Sweden proved too strong for a side managed by Pavel Sadyrin but they did make a

Russia narrowly lost out
to Mexico in the 2017
Confederations Cup

little bit of history in beating Cameroon 6-1 in the group stages, Russia's maiden victory in the finals as a sovereign country.

The nation has qualified twice since their American adventure. The 2002 finals in Japan and South Korea yielded another win, this time over Tunisia, but their latest World Cup in Brazil in 2014 was a sobering one. A draw with South Korea in their opening Group G fixture was promising enough but defeat to Belgium and another draw with Algeria sent the side home early without a win to their name.

Expectations of World Cup host nations, however, are always high and 2018 will be no exception as Stanislav Cherchesov's side aim to make the most of home advantage. At 65th in the Fifa standings when the finals draw was made the team were the lowest ranked of the 32 teams in the tournament but the Russian Football Union has publicly stated that an appearance in the last four is the minimum requirement of Cherchesov and his squad. However, having not been required to qualify it is difficult to accurately gauge exactly at what level the national team is playing.

Cherchesov won 39 caps in goal for Russia between 1992 and 2002. He got the job in August 2016, replacing Leonid Slutsky, after Russia failed to win any of their three group games against Wales, England or Slovakia in France at Euro 2016 and subsequent results under the 54-year-old have painted something of a mixed picture.

Russia's 2017 Confederations Cup campaign on home soil was respectable enough. A 2-0 victory over New Zealand in Saint Petersburg was a positive start and there was certainly no disgrace in the 1-0 defeat to Portugal and the 2-1 loss to Mexico that followed. Undeniably, Cherchesov's side acquitted themselves well in front of their own fans.

The friendlies under the new regime have been less consistent. Defeats to Costa Rica and Qatar in 2016 set alarm bells ringing and confidence was not exactly restored the following year when they were beaten by the Ivory Coast in Krasnodar in March and then held 1-1 by Iran in Kazan in October.

There were, however, highlights in 2017 to give the supporters reason for optimism. A 3-3 draw with the highly rated Belgians in Sochi was secured thanks to an injury-time winner from Rostov striker Aleksandr Bukharov and there was more cause for cheer in

November when Russia battled to another 3-3 draw with a marquee side, this time Spain in Saint Petersburg.

More good news for Cherchesov and Russia's hopes for 2018 came with the draw for the finals in Moscow. The hosts were placed in Group A with Saudi Arabia, Egypt and Uruguay, and while all three nations are worthy opponents Russia breathed an enormous sigh of relief as they avoided one of the tournament's genuine heavyweights.

The hosts kick-off the tournament against the Saudis in Moscow on 14 June, and should they be able to secure three points in the Luzhniki Stadium144 million Russians will inevitably start dreaming of their team reaching the knockout stages for the first time in the country's history.

The Kazan Arena, complete
with Russia 2018 branding

The 2018 World Cup promises to be the most spectacular yet, with millions of travelling fans able to sample everything Russia has to offer — especially their obvious love of hats...

THINGS CAN ONLY GET BETTER

After humiliation at the 2014 World Cup and Euro 2016, the Three Lions head to Russia on the back of a convincing qualifying campaign, raising hopes that the team are ready to restore national pride.

England supporters have become wearily accustomed to disappointment in recent years. The team's failure to get out of the group stages at the World Cup in Brazil in 2014, followed by the infamous defeat to Iceland in the European Championships in France two years later, was the bitterest of pills to swallow. However, as the Three Lions prepare for their 15th appearance in the World Cup finals, there's a cautious sense England may just have turned a corner.

Few but the most optimistic of fans expect England to be crowned world champions in Russia. Gareth Southgate's side remain very much a work in progress but the green shoots of recovery have undoubtedly been in evidence since the

England manager Gareth Southgate has yet to taste defeat in a competitive match

England's World Cup qualification was nothing if not comfortable. Eight wins and two draws in 10 games in Group F saw the side reach the finals without any undue alarm and they booked their place in Russia with a game to spare after Harry Kane's injury-time winner against Slovenia at Wembley in October.

England conceded just three goals in qualifying – only Spain could boast a similarly miserly defensive record in Europe – and although the Three Lions had been equally dominant en route to the finals of 2014, the renewed optimism generated by the solid 2018 qualifying campaign was warmly welcomed by supporters after the team's recent setbacks in major tournaments.

47-year-old was appointed manager in 2016. The Three Lions are yet to roar but England have at least regained some of their bite under their new boss.

Southgate's elevation from England's Under-21 coach to the top job came in the wake of the sacking of Sam Allardyce in September after one solitary game in charge. Southgate's initial four-game stint as caretaker manager produced two wins – including a 3-0 demolition of Scotland at Wembley – and two draws and in November the Football Association handed the former Crystal Palace, Aston Villa and Middlesbrough defender the managerial reins on a full-time basis.

Progress under Southgate since then has been steady rather than spectacular but his team have proven a tough one to beat. Their goalless draw with the world champions Germany at the end of 2017 followed – four days later – by the same result against Brazil underlined a growing sense of confidence within the England ranks.

The draw for the World Cup finals made in December was undoubtedly kind to England. Belgium in the final fixture of Group G will be a stern examination of the side's resolve and ability but Panama and Tunisia cannot boast the same pedigree, and although England have of late become masters in losing to supposedly weaker opposition at major events it could have been a significantly more daunting draw for Southgate's troops.

England could – perhaps should – go into the Belgium fixture in Kaliningrad on the back of two victories and with progress already secured to the knockout stages. Such a scenario would only ease the pressure on what will inevitably be an inexperienced squad and potentially afford them the freedom to go out and express themselves.

"We cannot go to a World Cup and not try to win it," Southgate said after the draw was made. "We've got to attempt to win each game, be as prepared as we can be, and see how far we can go. Of course a lot of these

Manchester United prodigy Marcus Rashford will be looking to push Harry Kane hard for a spot up front

players are going to peak in two to four years' time, but we can't just write off the tournament. I don't think anyone in England would accept that.

"Our last two tournaments have sadly been a disappointment. We've got to remember where we are starting from with this group of young players. But equally they're fiercely ambitious, everything is ahead of them and it's certainly not for me to put a limit on their expectations.

"In the past we have become unstuck against teams we'd perhaps be expected to beat, and at times we have played really well against teams that might be seeded higher than us.

"There is enough tension around tournaments anyway without the manager adding to that. It's important for the players to feel relaxed on a day-to-day basis. You are trying to maintain some normality around the bubble that is the World Cup. That's not always easy, but I think we have a good culture within the team, a group of players who really enjoy each others' company."

Southgate is acutely aware of the pressures of tournament football having played in the 1998 World Cup in France, as well as the finals of the European Championships in both 1996 – when England reached the semi-finals – and again in Belgium and the Netherlands four years later.

He played every minute of every match on home soil in Euro '96 only to suffer the agony of missing the decisive spot kick in the penalty shoot-out against Germany in the last four showdown at Wembley. Few have more first-hand knowledge of the potential highs and lows of international football.

The manager will need every ounce of his hard-won experience. His current England squad is a young one, albeit with clear potential, but a World Cup is an unforgiving environment and they will have precious little time to acclimatise to what is the biggest stage of their careers.

England's recent defensive record is formidable and in Kyle Walker, Danny Rose, Nathaniel Clyne, Ryan Bertrand and Kieran Trippier, Southgate has a glut of attacking full-backs. With the exception of Gary Cahill, however, the centre-backs are relatively unproven and much could depend on whether John Stones can translate his impressive club form at Manchester City under Pep Guardiola to England duty.

Perhaps the most glaring gap in the squad is the lack of a truly world-class central midfield playmaker. Jordan Henderson and Eric Dier have proven themselves dogged holding players, and while there's pace and guile further forward with the likes of Raheem Sterling, Dele Alli and Alex Oxlade-Chamberlain, England supporters could be forgiven for yearning for more creative spark in the middle of the pitch.

Injury deprived Southgate of the services of Adam Lallana for much of the first 12 months of his England reign, and if the talented Liverpool man can stay fit between now and the start of the World Cup his renewed presence in the starting XI could go a long way to addressing the problem.

Up front much rests on the young shoulders of Harry Kane. However, the Premier League's top scorer for two successive seasons still remains something of an international rookie and although his strike rate of 12 goals in his first 23 appearances for his country is far from shabby, he is not yet in the same bracket as the established international strikers whom he will, he'll hope, be vying with for the Golden Boot in Russia. The number of games played by Marcus Rashford for Manchester United in the build-up to the tournament could also prove a key factor in how far England are able to progress.

Southgate could yet spring a few surprises when he names his squad for 2018 given that he has plenty of hugely exciting youngsters on the fringe of his first team. Michael Keane, Joe Gomez, Ruben Loftus-Cheek, Tammy Abraham and Dominic Solanke all impressed when given the opportunity towards the end of 2017 and any one of them could yet emerge as a wildcard pick and make their mark in Russia. The debate whether Joe Hart remains England's first choice goalkeeper after winning 75 caps will rumble on, however, but Southgate will not lose any sleep over the quality of his potential younger successors, Jack Butland and Fraser Forster.

The impact the Three Lions can make in Russia will of course be partly dictated by form and fitness and not just the guidance the manager can provide, but Southgate can at least rest easy following the public assurance from the Football Association that he will keep his job even if his side fail to record a single victory.

That means Southgate has the luxury of keeping one eye on the future without the threat of the sack hanging over him, and given that England were toothless and winless in Brazil in 2014 expectations are not stratospheric.

The Three Lions are on a journey and for now Russia looks like a stop en route – albeit a potentially thrilling one – rather than the final destination.

Can England make it a treble after their youngsters triumphed in both the recent Under-17 (top) and Under-20 World Cups (above)?

Hotshot Spurs striker
Harry Kane scores
against France in a
friendly in June 2017

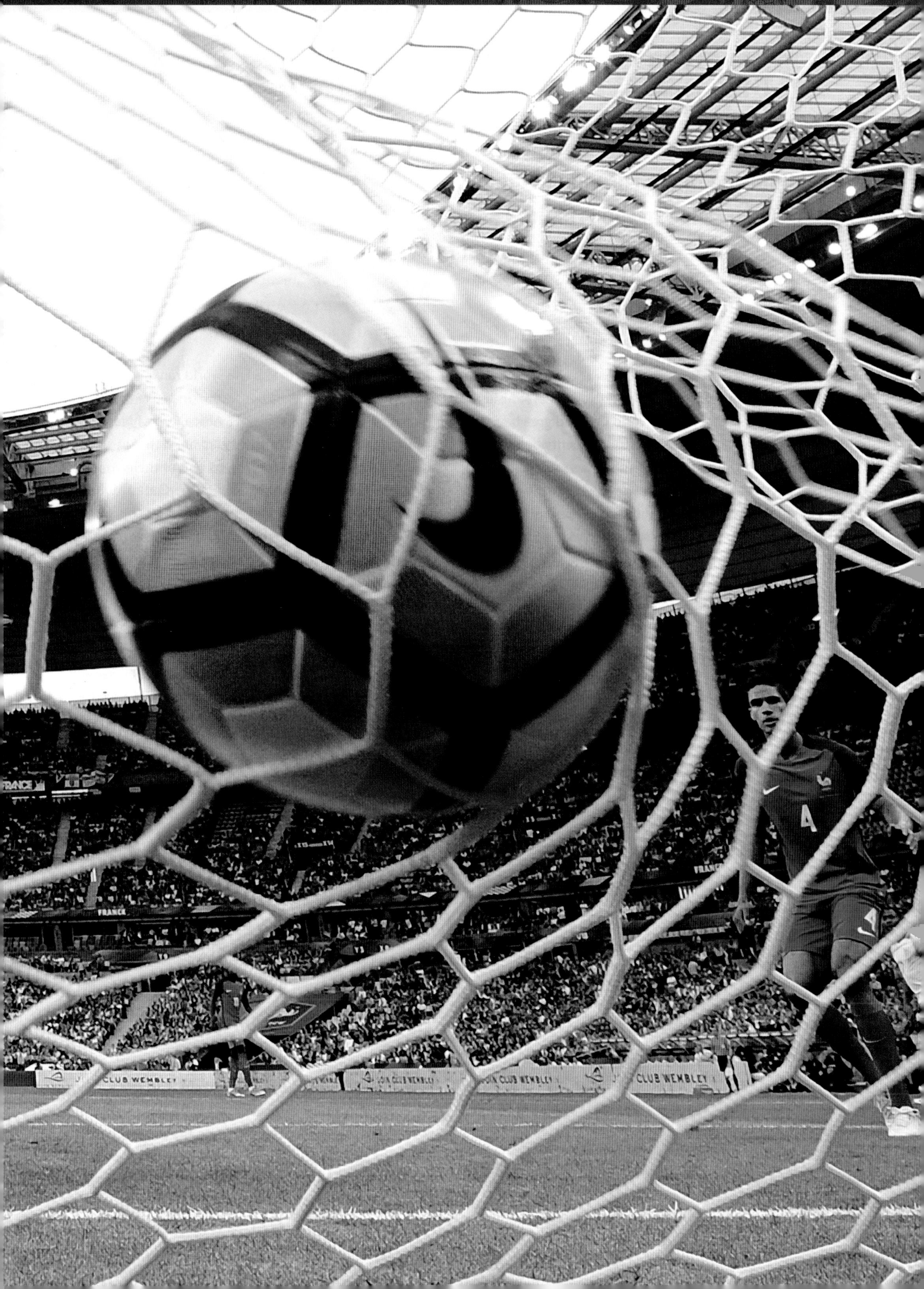
FRANCE
CLUB WEMBLEY
JOIN CLUB WEMBLEY
CLUB WEMBLEY
4

THE OPPOSITION

Familiar foes from the 1998 World Cup, unknown rivals from Central America and a European side bursting with talented players plying their trade in the Premier League, England's Group G opponents offer an eclectic and fascinating challenge.

TUNISIA V ENGLAND
Monday 18 June
7pm, BBC

One of five African teams heading to Russia, Tunisia have a respectable recent World Cup pedigree having qualified for three successive tournaments between 1998 and 2006, and although they were conspicuous by their absence at the last two tournaments the Eagles of Carthage will be no pushover.

Their Group G clash with England at the Volgograd Arena is a repeat of the meeting between the two nations in Marseille during the group stages of the 1998 finals, a game the Three Lions won 2-0 in the Stade Velodrome, and the 2018 reunion promises another fascinating encounter.

Tunisia booked their place in Russia in relative comfort after they topped Group A in the final round of CAF qualifying, unbeaten in six games home and away against DR Congo, Libya and Guinea. They were joint second top scorers with 11 goals, and their performances in 2016 and 2017 saw the North Africans rise to 27th in the Fifa world rankings, although they also went out to Burkina Faso at the quarter-final stage of the 2017 Africa Cup of Nations.

While the majority of the squad are based in the country, Tunisia will be looking to one of their overseas players, Youssef Msakni of the Qatari club Al-Duhail, for attacking inspiration after he top scored in the third round of qualifying. Mskani is the most prolific player in the current squad with 14 international goals up to the end of 2017, and will likely need to fire on all cylinders in Russia if the Eagles are to entertain any hope of progressing from the group phase for the first time in their history.

Manager Nabil Maaloul is in his second spell in charge of the national team after winning 74 caps for the country as a midfielder, and is fresh from a three-year stint as the head coach of Kuwait.

Tunisia will pose a definite challenge in England's opening fixture

ENGLAND V PANAMA
Sunday 24 June
1pm, BBC

England have never played Panama, and much else will also be new to the Central Americans in Russia in 2018 given it is the first time they've reached the World Cup finals. Known as La Marea Roja ('The Red Tide'), Panama first entered qualifying ahead of the 1978 tournament and have now finally achieved their goal at the 11th time of asking.

They booked their place in Russia in dramatic style with a 2-1 victory over Costa Rica in October in their final fixture courtesy of an 88th-minute goal from defender Roman Torres. The result meant the Panamanians edged out Honduras to the all-important third place in the group on goal difference and confirmed the nation as finalists for the first time in their history.

Panama (in red) are heading to the finals for the first time in their history

The team may have no World Cup experience but the manager, 62-year-old Colombian Hernan Dario Gomez is well acquainted with the finals having taken his native country to France in 1998, and Ecuador to Japan and South Korea four years later. Neither side made it to the knockout stages, but both teams did at least register one victory apiece.

Gomez was appointed Panama's manager in 2014 and he has moulded his side into an image of himself as a player. The Colombian was an industrious defensive midfielder by trade and his side, ranked 56th in the world at the end of 2017, are all about keeping things tight at the back.

As a result they conceded 10 times in 10 games in the final group phase of CONCACAF qualifying but, conversely, they were relatively ineffective at the other end of the pitch, scoring only nine goals in those 10 outings.

Torres is the team's main man, playing his club football in the American MLS for Seattle Sounders. He's been part of the Panama squad since his debut back in 2005 and in November 2016 won his 100th cap for his country in a goalless draw with Mexico in a World Cup qualifier.

ENGLAND V BELGIUM
Thursday 28 June
7pm, ITV

The fifth best side on the planet according to the Fifa rankings when the draw for the finals was made in late 2017, Belgium are currently blessed with a golden generation of talent and will surely prove to be England's toughest opponents by some distance when the two sides meet in Kaliningrad Stadium.

The Red Devils eased effortlessly into the finals in Russia with a near perfect record in qualification – nine wins and a draw – and scored 43 goals in the process, and there's star quality in every department of Roberto Martinez's squad.

Eden Hazard is the first amongst equals, however. The mercurial playmaker is a devastating force going forward on his day and although England's defence should know all about the threat he poses after his six seasons with Chelsea, forewarned is not always forearmed.

With as many as 18 of the current Belgian squad plying their trade in the Premier League, the clash in Kaliningrad in June will have a distinct derby feel to it and the side able to spring the biggest tactical surprise despite the pervading sense of familiarity could gain a key advantage.

Belgium are the stronger side than England on recent form and reputation, but the Three Lions do have a significant historical edge over them with just one defeat in normal time across the 21 fixtures between the two teams. That sole success for the Belgians came back in 1936, while England have won three of the last five encounters – although the 0-0 draw in 1998's King Hassan II International Cup in Morocco saw Belgium ultimately claim the spoils 4-3 on penalties.

Martinez's side flattered to deceive at both the 2014 World Cup and Euro 2016 despite their pre-tournament reputation, but with Kevin de Bruyne, Romelu Lukaku and Christian Benteke to supplement Hazard's well-documented attacking threat, combined with a back four likely to feature Jan Vertonghen, Vincent Kompany and Toby Alderweireld, they are a side bursting with potential match winners.

England will be wary of star Belgium striker Romelu Lukaku

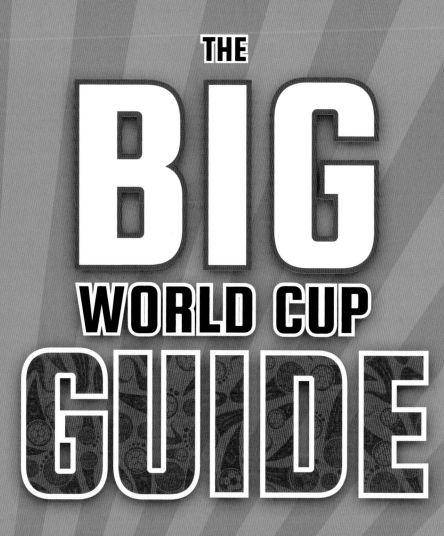

THE BIG WORLD CUP GUIDE

CONTENTS

DESTINATION RUSSIA

Featuring 11 host cities spread across the vast and diverse expanses of Russia that stretch from Asia to Eastern Europe, the 64 matches of the World Cup will be played out in 12 venues, several of which have been purpose-built for the eagerly anticipated tournament.

When football fans from across the globe descend on Russia for the 21st edition of the World Cup, they will be greeted by a dozen state-of-the-art stadia that the organisers are confident will provide the perfect backdrop for the beautiful game's greatest tournament.

Russia has spent billions to ensure its grounds are fit for purpose and ready in time, and with distinct architectural visions for each of the venues the competition promises to offer the estimated 2.5 million supporters who are expected to attend the tournament an unrivalled match day experience. The jewel in the crown is the 81,000-capacity Luzhniki Stadium in the capital, Moscow.

Originally opened in 1956 and the chief venue for the 1980 Summer Olympic Games, the iconic ground has undergone a major upgrade since Russia was confirmed as the host nation and will stage the World Cup final on 15 July.

It cost the hosts £305 million to remodel the stadium, and while the interior of the ground has undergone a complete modernisation – including the removal of the athletics track – its exterior facade has been left untouched to help preserve Luzhniki's long and proud history.

The second biggest venue for 2018 is the Saint Petersburg Stadium, a brand new ground that boasts a retractable roof and sliding grass pitch and will be able to accommodate around 68,000 spectators during the competition. It has been designed by Japanese architect Kisho Kurokawa to resemble a spaceship and is a modified and enlarged version of his previous creation, the acclaimed Toyota Stadium in Japan. The ground has already hosted the opening and closing matches of the 2017 Confederations Cup, and once the World Cup is finished it will serve as the home of Zenit St Petersburg.

Eight of the remaining stadia boast capacities of between 40,000 and 50,000, the largest of which is the Fisht Stadium in Sochi. Nestled by the Black Sea, it's the most southerly ground to be pressed into service for 2018 and was originally constructed to stage the opening and closing ceremonies of the 2014 Winter Olympics. It can hold more than 47,00 fans and will stage six games in total, including one of the quarter-finals. In doing so, Fisht will join the Stadio Olimpico in Turin, Italy, as one of only two venues ever to have hosted both the Winter Olympics and the World Cup.

The remaining seven grounds in this range are the Spartak Stadium, the Samara Arena, the Nizhny Novgorod Stadium and the Volgograd, Mordovia, Kazan and Rostov Arenas, which have a combined capacity of more than 315,000 between them.

The Spartak Stadium is the second ground in Moscow. It's the home of Spartak Moscow and is the only 2018 venue that was built solely utilising money from its parent club rather than investment from the Russian government. The ground has a stunning 24.5-metre high sculpture of the Roman gladiator Spartacus in a square outside the venue in celebration of the origins of the club's name.

The two smallest venues for 2018 are the Kaliningrad Stadium, in the west, which holds 35,212 people, and the slightly larger Ekaterinburg Arena in the east of the country which boasts a capacity of 35,696 and a history that dates back to 1957. It is currently home to club side FC Ural.

Many of the grounds will see their overall capacity reduced after the World Cup but there are legacy plans in place for all but one of the 12, ensuring Russia will reap the benefits of its huge investment in the tournament long after the fans have left and the new world champions have been crowned.

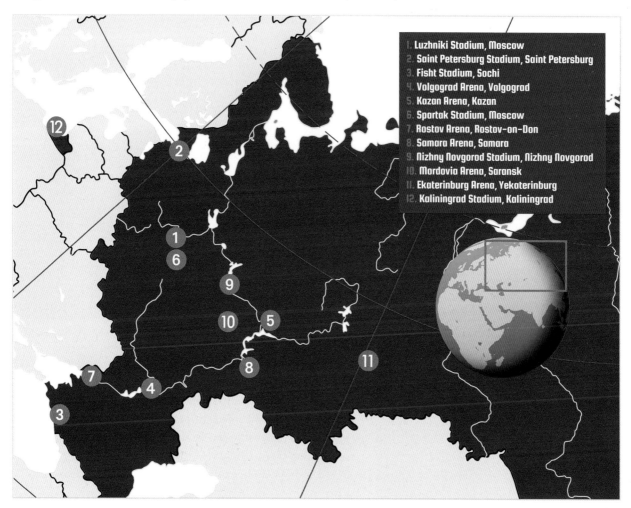

1. Luzhniki Stadium, Moscow
2. Saint Petersburg Stadium, Saint Petersburg
3. Fisht Stadium, Sochi
4. Volgograd Arena, Volgograd
5. Kazan Arena, Kazan
6. Spartak Stadium, Moscow
7. Rostov Arena, Rostov-on-Don
8. Samara Arena, Samara
9. Nizhny Novgorod Stadium, Nizhny Novgorod
10. Mordovia Arena, Saransk
11. Ekaterinburg Arena, Yekaterinburg
12. Kaliningrad Stadium, Kaliningrad

LUZHNIKI STADIUM ①
MOSCOW

Capacity: 81,000*
First built: 1956
Matches: 7

Officially reopened when Russia played Argentina in a friendly in November 2017 following a major refurbishment, the ground has seen the stands moved closer to its hybrid grass pitch and two extra tiers added to increase capacity in preparation for the World Cup. The venue for the 2008 Champions League final between Manchester United and Chelsea, the stadium has over the years been home to Moscow's Spartak, CSKA and Torpedo clubs but will be the new full-time base for the Russian national football team after the tournament.

SAINT PETERSBURG STADIUM ②
SAINT PETERSBURG

Capacity: 68,134*
First built: 2017
Matches: 7

Built on the site of the old 110,000-capacity Kirov Stadium on Krestovsky Island, the new ground will host seven games in 2018, including a semi-final and the third place play-off game. The stadium was officially christened when Russia took on New Zealand in the 2017 Confederations Cup and it also hosted that tournament's final between Chile and world champions Germany. The imposing seven-storey venue is 79 metres high and has been selected to stage three group stage matches and a quarter-final clash as part of Euro 2020's revamped format.

The Fisht Stadium helped put Sochi on the map when it was the centrepiece of the 2014 Winter Olympics, and it was reborn three years later when it staged four games during the 2017 Confederations Cup. It cost £350 million to originally build the venue and subsequently convert it into a football ground. It will host six World Cup matches, the standout fixture being the Group B Iberian derby between Portugal and Spain. The post World Cup future of the stadium, however, is unclear as Sochi does not currently have a local club ready to move in.

FISHT STADIUM 3
SOCHI

Capacity: 47,659*
First built: 2014
Matches: 6

Located on the site of the former 32,120-capacity Central Stadium, the roofline of the new ground had to be designed so it did not obscure the view of Volgograd's famous 'The Motherland Calls' sculpture, which commemorates the Battle of Stalingrad that took place during the Second World War. England will be in town to play Tunisia in June, and the stadium will also host three further group games. After the tournament FC Rotor Volgograd will move into a ground that is particularly striking thanks to its open metal lattice structure all around the exterior.

VOLGOGRAD ARENA 4
VOLGOGRAD

Capacity: 45,568*
First built: 2018
Matches: 4

KAZAN ARENA (5)
KAZAN

Capacity: 45,379*
First built: 2013
Matches: 6

The first of Russia's new stadiums to be completed when it opened in 2013, the Kazan Arena boasts the largest outdoor HD screen in Europe and was designed by the same firm responsible for Wembley Stadium and the Emirates Stadium in London. It demonstrated its versatility when it hosted events during the World Aquatics Championships courtesy of two temporary pools and was also one of the grounds used during the 2017 Confederations Cup. After 2018 the stadium will continue to be home to Russian Premier League side Rubin Kazan.

SPARTAK STADIUM (6)
MOSCOW

Capacity: 45,360*
First built: 2014
Matches: 5

Built on the site of a former airfield in the Tushino district of the city, the Spartak Stadium took four years to build and it held its first game in 2014 when Spartak welcomed Red Star Belgrade. The exterior of the ground is designed to resemble giant chain mail and evokes the club's famous red and white logo. After 2018 and the venue's four group stage fixtures and one Round of 16 match, there are plans in place to transform the surrounding area into a major residential development.

Excavation work for the stadium began in 2013 and saw five unexploded Second World War shells unearthed in the process. This discovery proved only a temporary setback, however, and the ground will be ready to host five games during the tournament. Located on the southern bank of the picturesque River Don, local Premier League club FC Rostov will take up residence at the stadium when the World Cup is concluded, and a host of new leisure facilities and housing developments are already planned to be added to the site.

ROSTOV ARENA 7
ROSTOV-ON-DON

Capacity: 45,000*
First built: 2018
Matches: 5

Russia will face Uruguay in their third and final Group A fixture in Samara. The ground will boast a spectacular glass dome that is designed to evoke the area's pivotal role in the Russian space programme. Work began on the ground in 2014 and once the World Cup is over it will become home to Russian National League side Krylya Sovetov. Construction cost approximately £230 million and the ground will host one Round of 16 match and one quarter-final fixture.

SAMARA ARENA 8
SAMARA

Capacity: 44,918*
First built: 2018
Matches: 6

NIZHNY NOVGOROD STADIUM 9
NIZHNY NOVGOROD

Capacity: 44,899*
First built: 2018
Matches: 6

Featuring an expansive white roof supported by columns, the stadium is one of the most eye-catching Russia has to offer and affords fans views of the Oka and Volga rivers as well as the nearby Alexander Nevsky Cathedral. The ground has been selected as the venue for one of the tournament's quarter-finals, but England fans will be more preoccupied with the prospect of the Three Lions' group clash with Panama. Second tier side Olimpiyets Nizhny Novgorod will move in when the World Cup is done and dusted despite an average home gate of around 1,000 fans.

MORDOVIA ARENA 10
SARANSK

Capacity: 44,442*
First built: 2018
Matches: 4

With a population of around 300,000, Saransk was a surprise choice as a World Cup venue but its new stadium is undoubtedly striking, an oval construction which will be decorated with the bright orange, red and white colours traditionally associated with the art of the region. Large parts of the ground are temporary to allow its capacity to be reduced back to 25,000 when FC Mordovia Saransk move in after the tournament. The reconfiguration of the venue post-2018 will also see indoor volleyball, basketball and tennis courts built.

The revamped stadium in the foothills of the Ural mountains has enjoyed a varied history since it was opened in the 1950s – including hosting world championship speed skating – and although it has undergone many refurbishments over the years its original facade has been left untouched. Its most recent update saw 12,000 temporary seats installed on scaffolding in readiness for the first of its four scheduled World Cup matches, the Group A clash between Egypt and Uruguay. The ground will remain the home of FC Ural Yekaterinburg after the tournament.

EKATERINBURG ARENA
YEKATERINBURG

11

Capacity: 35,696*
First built: 1957
Matches: 4

The venue for England's Group G showdown with Belgium, Kaliningrad is a unique location cut off from the rest of Russia and surrounded by Poland and Lithuania. It cost £220 million to build the stadium, and after the 2018 finals a section of the roof will be removed and the overall capacity reduced as it becomes a 25,000 all-seater ground and home to FC Baltika Kaliningrad, as well as a regular concert and entertainment venue.

KALININGRAD STADIUM
KALININGRAD

12

Capacity: 35,212*
First built: 2018
Matches: 4

* Capacity figures indicate the anticipated gross capacity for the stadiums in their finished state. The stadiums' official capacity for the 2018 World Cup will be lower due to World Cup-specific requirements.

RUSSIA

As the hosts of this summer's finals Russia will be desperate to do well. Their record in tournament football in recent years is pretty poor but they have the advantage of being one of the eight top seeds and backed by their passionate fans they will fight to the last. Despite being the lowest ranked country at the tournament, their three group opponents can each expect a tough game.

Having enjoyed automatic qualification for the finals, Russia have mainly played friendlies since their disappointing exit from Euro 2016, after which former international goalkeeper Stanislav Cherchesov took over as coach. The exception came in June 2017 when the Russians hosted the Confederations Cup, but they largely failed to impress. Since then, though, the Russians have enjoyed some encouraging results in friendlies, including a 4-2 win against South Korea and a 3-3 draw with Spain.

It's quite probable that Russia's entire starting XI at the World Cup will be comprised of home-based players. Among the more familiar names are goalkeeper and captain Igor Akinfeev of CSKA Moscow, a veteran with over 100 caps; former Chelsea wing-back Yuri Zhirkov, now of Zenit Saint Petersburg; and goalscoring midfielder Alan Dzagoev, also of CSKA. Perhaps, though, Russia's most interesting player is Aleksandr Golovin, a young creative midfielder who has attracted a lot of attention from leading European clubs. As those recent friendly results indicate, Russia are certainly not toothless in attack either and in Krasnodar's Fedor Smolov and Zenit's Dmitriy Poloz have a pair of sharp-shooting strikers who can trouble any backline.

However, there are serious doubts about a defence which often struggles to keep clean sheets, and it is hard to see Russia getting any further than the last 16 – if, indeed, they progress out of their group at all.

> **"I cannot say if I am happy or not after the draw. The group is what it is."**
>
> Russia coach
> Stanislav Cherchesov

THE GAFFER
STANISLAV CHERCHESOV

Bald, thickset and moustachioed, Stanislav Cherchesov could easily pass as a Bond villain's burly henchman, but beneath his dour exterior the Russian coach has a keen football brain and he will be determined that the hosts perform to their best at this summer's finals.

Appointed as successor to Leonid Slutsky after Russia's disappointing showing at Euro 2016, the 54-year-old has shaken up a stale squad, introducing a batch of younger players and successfully switching to a more attractive 3-5-2 formation. Nonetheless, the evidence of the 2017 Confederations Cup, where Russia came third in their group after losing to both Mexico and Portugal, suggests his stated aim of reaching the semi-finals of the World Cup will be well beyond his workmanlike side.

Although this is his first job in international football, Cherchesov is an experienced club manager having enjoyed stints with, among others, Spartak Moscow, Dynamo Moscow and Legia Warsaw, with whom he won the Polish domestic double in 2016.

A former goalkeeper, Cherchesov played 39 times for Russia and was a member of his country's World Cup squads in both 1994 and 2002. At club level he won the Russian Premier League title with Spartak Moscow in 1992 and 1993.

KEY PLAYER

IGOR AKINFEEV

A goalkeeper with cat-like reflexes who has been compared to the legendary Lev Yashin, Igor Akinfeev will be Russia's captain at the finals this summer. There's every likelihood he will be a busy figure between the posts, but if the 31-year-old is on top form his country's chances of at least progressing to the last 16 will be greatly enhanced.

Akinfeev made his international debut as an 18-year-old in 2004 and has now won over 100 caps. His best moment with his country came in 2008 when Russia reached the semi-finals of the European Championships before losing to eventual winners Spain.

A one-club man, Akinfeev has spent his entire career with CSKA Moscow, helping the one-time Soviet army team win six league titles, six Russian Cups and the UEFA Cup in 2005. Even more impressively, perhaps, he has kept more clean sheets in club football than any other Russian goalkeeper in history. A few more will do Russia's chances of progressing the power of good.

ONE TO WATCH
ALEKSANDR GOLOVIN

Considered one of the brightest prospects in world football, CSKA Moscow's Aleksandr Golovin is a creative midfielder who combines skill and flair with tenacity and aggression. Little wonder, then, that the 21-year-old has been linked with a host of top clubs, including Arsenal, Chelsea and Barcelona, all of whom were reported to be planning big-money bids during the January 2018 transfer window.

Golovin has already won international silverware, helping Russia claim the 2013 European Under-17 Championship following a penalty shoot-out victory against Italy in the final in Slovakia. Two years later he was part of the Russian team which reached the 2015 Under-19 final, but lost 2-0 to Spain in Greece. In the same year, the talented youngster made his full international debut, coming on as a second-half sub in a friendly against Belarus and scoring in a 4-2 win.

A regular for CSKA since 2015, Golovin helped his club win the Russian Premier League the following year and his deft skills on the ball allied to his hardworking approach have made him a firm favourite with fans of the Russian giants.

TACTICS BOARD

WIDE DELIVERY

Since taking over as Russia coach in 2016, Stanislav Cherchesov has introduced a 3-5-2 system with the emphasis on getting the ball wide to wing-backs who can deliver dangerous crosses into the box.

Former Chelsea man Yuri Zhirkov, now with Zenit Saint Petersburg, is likely to be the player hugging the left touchline, while Spartak Moscow's Aleksandr Samedov is the favourite to occupy the right wing-back slot. In central midfield, the technically gifted Aleksandr Golovin of CSKA Moscow is the key man, his ability on the ball allowing him to thread through pinpoint passes for the twin strikers, Krasnodar's Fedor Smolov and Zenit's Dmitriy Poloz – with the experienced Aleksandr Kokorin, also of Zenit, another potential forward option.

In defence, CSKA Moscow's Viktor Vasin is the central figure in a decidedly rugged back three, supported by Rubin Kazan's Fedor Kudryashov and Spartak Moscow's Georgi Dzhikiya. Behind them, Igor Akinfeev is a highly capable and very experienced goalkeeper.

RUSSIA AT THE WORLD CUP

• Competing as the Soviet Union, Russia made their first appearance at the finals in 1958 in Sweden. After finishing in joint second place in their group with England, the Soviets then beat Walter Winterbottom's team 1-0 in a play-off before losing 2-0 to the hosts in the quarter-finals just two days later.

• **Inspired by legendary goalkeeper Lev Yashin, Russia made their best-ever showing at the finals in 1966 in England. After topping their group and then beating Hungary 2-1 in the quarter-finals, the Russians went down 2-1 to West Germany in the semi-final at Goodison Park.**

• Four years later Russian striker Anatoliy Puzach became the first substitute to be used at the finals when he came on in the opening fixture, a boring 0-0 draw with hosts Mexico. The Soviets went on to reach the quarter-finals, where they lost 1-0 to Uruguay.

• **The Soviet Union were disqualified from the 1974 tournament after refusing to travel to Chile for the second leg of their inter-continental play-off. The Russians protested that the stadium in Santiago had been** used to torture political prisoners following a recent military coup.

• At the 1982 finals in Spain the Soviets pipped Scotland to second place in their group on goal difference following an exciting 2-2 draw between the teams in the final match. In the second group stage the Russians needed to beat Poland in Barcelona to reach the semi-finals but could only manage a 0-0 draw.

• **The Soviet Union began the 1986 finals in Mexico in fine style with a 6-0 hammering of Hungary. The Russians cruised into the last 16 where, despite a hat-trick from striker Igor Belanov, they lost 4-3 after extra-time to Belgium.**

• The country's first official appearance at the finals as Russia following the breakup of the Soviet Union was at USA '94. After defeats to Brazil and Sweden the Russians were eliminated but they took some consolation from their last game, a 6-1 hammering of Cameroon in which Oleg Salenko scored five goals.

• **Russia began the 2002 finals promisingly with a 2-0 defeat of Tunisia, before defeats to Japan and Belgium ended their dreams of going further in the competition.**

• At their last appearance in the finals in 2014 Russia again disappointed, collecting just two points from their three games.

The Soviet Union in action against hosts Mexico in 1970

PREVIOUS TOURNAMENTS

1930 Did not enter	1966 Fourth place	1994 Round 1
1934 Did not enter	1970 Quarter-finals	1998 Did not qualify
1938 Did not enter	1974 Disqualified	2002 Round 1
1950 Did not enter	1978 Did not qualify	2006 Did not qualify
1954 Did not enter	1982 Round 2	2010 Did not qualify
1958 Quarter-finals	1986 Round 2	2014 Round 1
1962 Quarter-finals	1990 Round 1	

SAUDI ARABIA

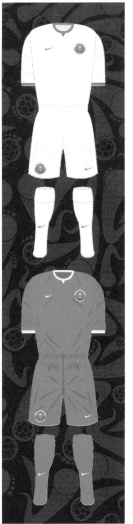

After playing in four consecutive World Cups between 1994 and 2006 Saudi Arabia missed the boat for the last two finals, so will simply be glad to back on board in Russia. Drawn in a tough group, their chances of causing an upset must be rated as slim, especially as they have lost the services of the manager, Dutchman Bert van Marwijk, who guided them through the qualification process.

Van Marwijk quit his post after failing to agree a new contract just days after Saudi Arabia clinched their place at the finals with a 1-0 home victory against group winners Japan in September 2017. He was replaced by Edgardo Bauza but the former Argentina boss lasted just five matches before he was sacked, and the managerial merry-go-round only ended when Juan Antonio Pizzi, a one-time Barcelona and Spain striker who led Chile to Copa America glory in 2016, took over the reins.

> "We're in the opening game and it will be difficult. It's a very balanced group."
>
> Saudi Arabia coach Juan Antonio Pizzi

The squad Pizzi has inherited is lacking in star names, but it is extremely tight-knit being drawn almost entirely from a handful of leading Saudi clubs. Among the most important players are veteran goalkeeper Waleed Abdullah of Al Nassr, uncompromising centre-back and captain Osama Hawsawi and Yahya Al-Shehri, a 27-year-old winger who became the most expensive player ever in Saudi football when he moved from Ettifaq to Al Nassr for £9.6 million in 2013.

Perhaps, though, the most influential figure in the Saudi team is Taiseer Al-Jassam of Al-Ahli. A technically gifted midfielder who loves to dribble and shoot from distance he will be at the heart of his side's best moves, but at the age of 33 may be past his best. Still, if Al-Jassam can provide the ammunition for prolific striker Mohammad Al-Sahlawi then 'Al-Suquor' (The Falcons) might yet confound the odds and claim a place in the knockout stages.

SAUDI ARABIA AT THE WORLD CUP

• Saudi Arabia didn't appear at the World Cup until 1994, but it proved to be a memorable experience, especially for Saaed Al-Owairan who scored a superb winner against Belgium after running half the length of the pitch. The goal took the Falcons through to the last 16, where they lost 3-1 to Sweden.

• Four years later, the Saudis fared less well, losing to both Denmark and hosts and eventual winners France before managing a face-saving 2-2 draw with South Africa.

• That, though, was a triumph compared to the Saudis' 2002 campaign. Their tournament opened disastrously with an 8-0 hammering at the hands of eventual finalists Germany and continued poorly with defeats to Cameroon (0-1) and the Republic of Ireland (0-3).

• Taking part in a fourth consecutive tournament in 2006, the Falcons were dramatically denied three points in their opening fixture when Tunisia equalised with virtually the last kick of the match to make the final score 2-2. A 4-0 thrashing against Ukraine followed before their chances of progressing further in the competition were snuffed out by a 1-0 loss to Spain.

PREVIOUS TOURNAMENTS

1930-54 Not a Fifa member	1982 Did not qualify	2010 Did not qualify
1958 Did not enter	1986 Did not qualify	2014 Did not qualify
1962 Did not enter	1990 Did not qualify	
1966 Did not enter	1994 Round 2	
1970 Did not enter	1998 Round 1	
1974 Did not enter	2002 Round 1	
1978 Did not qualify	2006 Round 1	

KEY PLAYER

MOHAMMAD AL-SAHLAWI

Few strikers will head to Russia in better goalscoring form than Saudi Arabia frontman Mohammad Al-Sahlawi, who was joint top scorer in the Asian qualification section with 16 goals.

A hard-running player who constantly harries defenders and likes to drop deep to link up play, Al-Sahlawi began his career with Saudi club Al-Qadisiya. In the 2007/08 season he was top scorer in the country's second flight, prompting big guns Al-Nassr to pay a then Saudi record fee of around £5 million for his services. In his first season with his new club he hit an impressive 21 goals in 36 games and was deservedly named Young Player of the Year. Al-Sahlawi has gone on to help his club win the Saudi league twice and in 2014 he scored the winner from the penalty spot in a 2-1 victory over arch rivals Al-Hilal in the final of the Crown Prince Cup.

Now 31, he made his international debut for Saudi Arabia in 2010 and has an extremely impressive goalscoring record for his country with 28 goals in 33 games.

43

EGYPT

Despite having won the Africa Cup of Nations a record seven times Egypt have only previously featured at two World Cup finals, in 1934 and 1990. Little wonder, then, that there were wild scenes in Cairo's iconic Tahrir Square when the Pharaohs booked their passage to Russia with a 2-1 home win against Congo, thousands of flag-waving fans lighting flares, letting off fireworks and blaring their car horns long into the night.

The jubilant mood in the nation was in stark contrast to the gloom-filled one in February 2012 when 74 fans of Cairo giants Al-Ahly were killed and more than 500 injured following a stadium riot in Port Said. The Egyptian government responded to the disaster by shutting down the domestic league for two seasons, making life extremely difficult for the national team.

However, a new, more positive era for Egypt began with the appointment of experienced Argentinian Hector Cuper as coach in 2015. Despite being criticised for his cautious approach and over-reliance on Liverpool striker Mohamed Salah, the former Valencia and Inter Milan boss raised spirits by leading the Pharaohs to the final of the 2017 Africa Cup of Nations, which they lost to Cameroon.

A bulwark of the side during good and bad times has been goalkeeper Essam El-Hadary, who has won over 150 caps and at 45 will hope to set a new record in Russia as the oldest player ever to appear at the finals. Apart from the brilliant Salah, who has set the Premier League alight in his first season at Anfield, other English-based players in the squad include Aston Villa right-back Ahmed Elmohamady, giant West Brom central defender Ahmed Hegazi, solid Arsenal defensive midfielder Mohamed Elneny and Stoke midfielder Ramadan Sobhi. Among the domestic-based contingent, meanwhile, perhaps the most important player for the Pharaohs is Al-Ahly defender Ahmed Fathy, a veteran with over 120 caps to his name.

> **"I can't quite say it is an easy or difficult group."**
> Egypt coach
> Hector Cuper

EGYPT AT THE WORLD CUP

• Egypt became the first African country ever to appear at the World Cup when they played Hungary in the first round in Naples in 1934. The Pharaohs did their continent proud, striker Abdulrahman Fawzi scoring twice in the first half before they eventually went down to a 4-2 defeat.

• Four years later Egypt refused to play a qualifier against Romania because the fixture was due to take place during the fasting month of Ramadan, and were promptly withdrawn from the competition by Fifa.

• The north Africans had to wait until 1990 before they featured at the finals again. In their opening match against reigning European champions the Netherlands on the Italian island of Sicily, Egypt performed superbly, fully deserving their 1-1 draw.

• After a 0-0 draw with the Republic of Ireland, Egypt started brightly in their final match against England in Sardinia and threatened to take the lead. In the end, however, a single headed goal by England's Mark Wright decided the encounter, leaving Egypt bottom of the group.

PREVIOUS TOURNAMENTS

1930 Did not enter	1966 Withdrew	1994 Did not qualify
1934 Round 1	1970 Did not enter	1998 Did not qualify
1938 Withdrew	1974 Did not qualify	2002 Did not qualify
1950 Did not enter	1978 Did not qualify	2006 Did not qualify
1954 Did not qualify	1982 Did not qualify	2010 Did not qualify
1958 Withdrew	1986 Did not qualify	2014 Did not qualify
1962 Withdrew	1990 Round 1	

KEY PLAYER

MOHAMED ELNENY

Frizzy-haired Arsenal midfielder Mohamed Elneny's ability to win tackles and start off attacks will be crucial to Egypt's chances of progressing out of an intriguing group in Russia. The 25-year-old is also capable of popping up with the occasional goal, as he demonstrated with a well-taken strike from a tight angle in the 2017 Africa Cup of Nations final against Cameroon.

After a number of years spent in the youth ranks of Al-Ahly, Elneny began his senior career with Cairo rivals El Mokawloon. In January 2013 he joined Basel, initially on loan, and won the Swiss Super League three times before securing a £7.4 million move to Arsenal three years later. In 2017 he became the first Egyptian ever to win the FA Cup when he came on as a late sub in the Gunners' 2-1 victory against London rivals Chelsea at Wembley.

Elneny first played for Egypt in 2011 and the following year featured for the Under-23 team at the London Olympics, helping the Pharaohs reach the quarter-finals where they lost to Japan. He is now approaching 60 caps for his country and will likely play a vital part in his side's campaign.

URUGUAY

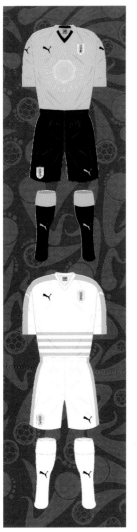

The smallest nation ever to win the World Cup, Uruguay lifted the trophy in both 1930 and 1950. The South Americans could be dark horses this summer in Russia too, partly because the draw has been kind to them but mainly due to the fact that in Paris Saint-Germain's Edinson Cavani and Barcelona's Luis Suarez they have two of the deadliest strikers in world football.

Cavani was the leading marksman in the CONMEBOL qualifying section with 10 goals as Uruguay came second in the group behind runaway leaders Brazil. However, it was far from plain sailing for 'La Celeste' who suffered three consecutive defeats at one point during their qualification campaign before a late rally booked their passage. Veteran coach Oscar Tabarez, who has used a wheelchair since being diagnosed with Guillain-Barre syndrome in 2016, made the brave decision of shaking up his side by introducing some young talented midfielders and the gamble paid off as Uruguay picked up form in the final straight.

> **"There are no easy matches, especially at the World Cup."**
> Uruguay coach
> Oscar Tabarez

The promising trio of Federico Valverde, Rodrigo Bentancur and Nahitan Nandez, all 21 or younger, have helped transform Uruguay from a rather dour unit into a highly entertaining one. If they can deliver the ammunition for Cavani and Suarez then the South Americans will be a force to be reckoned with, especially as their defence, led by wily skipper Diego Godin of Atletico Madrid, is extremely well-drilled. Goalkeeper Fernando Muslera of Galatasaray, who is approaching the 100-cap mark, is another huge asset to a team which appears to have the perfect blend of youth and experience.

Uruguay should have no problems qualifying from a comparatively weak group, but a potential clash with either Spain or Portugal in the Round of 16 looks extremely awkward and may end their hopes of a third World Cup triumph.

THE GAFFER
OSCAR TABAREZ

The longest-serving manager at this summer's finals, Oscar Tabarez has been the boss of Uruguay since 2006. He also had another stint as his country's coach between 1988 and 1990 and his total of 183 matches in charge of the South Americans is a world record.

Dubbed 'El Maestro' ('The Teacher') for a spell he had as a primary school teacher following the end of his modest playing career, the 70-year-old Tabarez has overseen an upsurge in Uruguay's fortunes following their failure to qualify for the 2006 World Cup in Germany. Four years later he guided them to fourth place at the finals in South Africa and in 2011 he led his team to victory in the Copa America final in Argentina. More recently, he has revamped an ageing side which failed to meet expectations at the last World Cup in Brazil, introducing a number of exciting young players to complement older stars like Luis Suarez and Edinson Cavani.

South American Coach of the Year in 2010 and 2011, Tabarez previously enjoyed a long career in club football, managing the likes of Cagliari, AC Milan, Boca Juniors and Penarol, with whom he won the Copa Libertadores way back in 1987.

KEY PLAYER

LUIS SUAREZ

A deadly penalty box poacher who can score from seemingly impossible angles, Luis Suarez is Uruguay's all-time top scorer with 49 goals.

Five of those strikes came at the previous two finals, but the 31-year-old's World Cup memories are not all happy. In South Africa in 2010 he was sent off in the quarter-final against Ghana after palming away a goalbound header, and then angered neutrals by describing the incident as 'the save of the tournament'. Four years later in Brazil he was again involved in controversy when he bit Italian defender Giorgio Chiellini, earning a four-month ban from Fifa. Incredibly, it was the third time in his career that he had been punished for biting an opponent.

Formerly with Ajax, Suarez joined Barcelona from Liverpool for £75 million in 2014 and the following year helped the Catalan giants win the Treble. In 2016 he won the European Golden Boot after another goal-filled La Liga season.

ONE TO WATCH
FEDERICO VALVERDE

A deep-lying central midfielder whose range of passing has seen him compared to Italian legend Andrea Pirlo, Federico Valverde is tipped to be one of the game's future stars. Still only 19, he has already impressed in the colours of Uruguay since winning his first cap in September 2017 and great things are expected of him in Russia this summer.

Nicknamed 'El Pajarito' ('The Little Bird') for his distinctive running style, Valverde came through the ranks of Montevideo giants Penarol to make his senior debut at just 17. His accomplished displays soon attracted the interest of the likes of Arsenal, Chelsea and Barcelona and in July 2016 he moved to Real Madrid, being assigned to the club's 'B' team, Castilla. The following year he joined La Liga outfit Deportivo La Coruna on loan.

In the summer of 2017 Valverde performed brilliantly at the Under-20 World Cup in South Korea, winning the Silver Ball award. Less happily, he was slammed by local fans for a 'racist' goal celebration, when he slanted his eyes with his fingers after scoring a penalty against Portugal.

TACTICS BOARD

SUPPLYING STAR STRIKERS

It's not so long ago that Uruguay's 4-4-2 formation regularly resembled 8-0-2 as the South Americans sought to pack their defence and hit high, hopeful balls from deep to their two world-class strikers Edinson Cavani and Luis Suarez.

However, in recent months coach Oscar Tabarez, while sticking to the same system, has introduced a lot more flair and creativity into his side in the shape of 19-year-old prodigy Federico Valverde, 20-year-old Juventus starlet Rodrigo Bentancur and 21-year-old Nahitan Nandez of Boca Juniors. Supported by the left-sided Cristian Rodriguez of Penarol, Uruguay's midfield is now more balanced, and the supply to their deadly duo up front has increased in both quality and quantity.

In defence, the South Americans remain steadfast and resolute, their gritty back four centred around the Atletico Madrid pair of captain Diego Godin and Jose Gimenez, with Porto's Maxi Pereira another longstanding mainstay at right-back.

URUGUAY AT THE WORLD CUP

• In 1930 Uruguay became the first winners of the World Cup when they beat neighbours Argentina 4-2 in the final in Montevideo. A bizarre dispute about which ball to use for the match was solved when the teams agreed to use an Argentinian ball in the first half and a Uruguayan one in the second half.

• Uruguay won the World Cup for a second time in 1950 when they came from behind to beat hosts Brazil 2-1 in the 'final' (it was actually the last match in a four-team final group). The match was watched by a crowd of 199,589 in the Maracana Stadium in Rio, the largest ever attendance at a football match.

• Four years later in Switzerland Uruguay hammered Scotland 7-0 – the Scots' worst ever defeat – on their way to the semi-finals, before losing 4-2 to Hungary.

• Uruguay reached the quarter-finals at the 1966 finals but were soundly trounced 4-0 by West Germany after having two players sent off at Hillsborough.

• The South Americans made it to the semi-finals once again in 1970 in Mexico. Up against their

Uruguay put four goals past erstwhile rivals Argentina during the 1930 final

old adversaries Brazil, Uruguay took the lead but eventually lost 3-1. Incredibly, and despite coming fourth, in their six matches at the tournament Uruguay only managed a measly four goals in total.

• The next four decades saw Uruguay make very little impact at the finals, and they even failed to qualify on five occasions. The South Americans' best showings at the tournament during this miserable period came in 1986 and 1990 when they reached the last 16 before losing to Argentina and Italy respectively.

• Uruguay finally returned to form at the 2010 finals in South Africa.

After two Luis Suarez goals saw off South Korea in the last 16, the South Americans met Ghana in the quarter-finals. With the scores tied at 1-1 deep into extra-time, Suarez palmed away a goalbound header and was sent off. However, Ghana missed the resulting penalty and Uruguay won the subsequent shoot-out. Their luck, however, ran out in the semi-finals when they lost 3-2 to Germany.

• At their last appearance at the finals in 2014 in Brazil, Uruguay got off to a wretched start with a shock 3-1 defeat to Costa Rica. However, they then beat Roy Hodgson's England side and Italy to reach the last 16 before going down 2-0 to Colombia.

PREVIOUS TOURNAMENTS

1930 Winners	1966 Quarter-finals	1994 Did not qualify
1934 Withdrew	1970 Fourth place	1998 Did not qualify
1938 Did not enter	1974 Round 1	2002 Round 1
1950 Winners	1978 Did not qualify	2006 Did not qualify
1954 Fourth place	1982 Did not qualify	2010 Fourth place
1958 Did not qualify	1986 Round 2	2014 Round 2
1962 Round 1	1990 Round 2	

PORTUGAL

After finally winning their first ever major tournament at Euro 2016 thanks to a surprise 1-0 victory over hosts France in the final, Portugal's confidence is at an all-time high. However, the odds must be against coach Fernando Santos successfully plotting another unlikely triumph in Russia, although it goes without saying that a side with the legendary Cristiano Ronaldo in their ranks must never be dismissed lightly.

Portugal demonstrated the mental strength that served them so well in France in their qualifying group, which turned into a straight duel for top spot with Switzerland. In the end, the Portuguese grabbed the prize, beating the Swiss 2-0 in in the final round of matches to head the group on goal difference.

Almost inevitably, Ronaldo was the team's main source of goals with 15, but AC Milan's Andre Silva chipped in with nine of his own to suggest that Portugal are not now quite as reliant on the Real Madrid superstar to be their match-winner as they once were. At the other end, the Portuguese were very solid, keeping clean sheets in seven of their 10 games. Santos prides himself on having a well-drilled defence and in former Real Madrid hatchetman Pepe, West Ham stopper Jose Fonte and Southampton's Cedric Soares he has intelligent players who can implement his plans. Behind them, Sporting Lisbon's Rui Patricio is an experienced goalkeeper who rarely makes mistakes. Meanwhile, in midfield Portugal have a good blend of tenacity and creativity, with Sporting Lisbon's William Carvalho providing the steel while Manchester City's Bernardo Silva and Monaco's stylish Joao Moutinho contribute an abundance of flair and guile.

With the latter pair in tandem, Portugal are now a more stylish outfit than when they triumphed in France, but have not lost their tactical nous and look a good bet to progress to at least the quarter-finals in Russia.

> **"It's a very deceptive and treacherous group. It's very difficult."**
> Portugal coach Fernando Santos

THE GAFFER
FERNANDO SANTOS

Portugal coach Fernando Santos wrote himself into the history books when he guided his country to their first ever major tournament success, the European Championships in 2016. The Lisbon-born boss deserved huge credit for the unexpected triumph, reducing his team's dependency on star striker Cristiano Ronaldo and instilling a disciplined tactical mentality in a group of players previously known for an off-the-cuff approach.

It wasn't the first time either that Santos had surpassed expectations with a relatively small football power. In a previous spell with Greece he took them to the quarter-finals of the 2012 European Championships and then the last 16 of the 2014 World Cup in Brazil – not bad for a nation which had never reached the knockout stage before. However, during Greece's defeat on penalties to Costa Rica his fiery temperament let him down and he was sent off for dissent, subsequently collecting a six-match ban from the dug-out.

In a lengthy managerial career spent entirely in Portugal and Greece the former Estoril and Maritimo defender managed a number of big clubs, including Porto, Benfica, Sporting Lisbon, AEK Athens and Panathinaikos. Santos' greatest success came with Porto, who he led to the league title in 1999.

KEY PLAYER

WILLIAM CARVALHO

One reason why Portugal only conceded four goals in their qualifying campaign was due to the presence in midfield of the towering William Carvalho, a one-man wall in front of his defence. However, the Sporting Lisbon star is not merely a destroyer, possessing the ability to start potentially dangerous attacks with his pinpoint passing and boundless energy.

Born in Angola, Carvalho came to Portugal as a child and joined the Sporting youth system aged 13. After loan spells with third-tier Fatima and Belgian club Cercle Brugge he established himself in the Lisbon giants' first team for whom his rugged and combative displays have attracted the interest of Premier League titans Arsenal and Liverpool.

Carvalho was first capped for Portugal in 2013 and two years later was named Player of the Tournament at the European Under-21 Championships in the Czech Republic despite missing the decisive penalty in the shoot-out in the final against Sweden.

ONE TO WATCH
ANDRE SILVA

While Portugal's opponents in Russia will need no warnings about the danger posed by the great Cristiano Ronaldo, they would be well-advised to keep a sharp eye on Andre Silva as well. The AC Milan striker was in prolific goalscoring form during the qualifiers, scoring an impressive total of nine goals including a first-half hat-trick in a 6-0 drubbing of minnows the Faroes Islands. More significantly, perhaps, he was also on target with a trademark close-range finish that wrapped up the vital 2-0 home win against Switzerland on the final day of the campaign which clinched Portugal's place in Russia.

Now 22, Silva began his career with Porto B before making his first-team debut in December 2015. The following year he scored twice against Braga in the Portuguese Cup final but still finished on the losing side. In the summer of 2017 he moved on to AC Milan for around £33 million, and in September that year scored a hat-trick in a 5-1 thrashing of Austria Vienna in the Europa League – the first treble by a Milan player in Europe for 11 years.

TACTICS BOARD

SOLID FIRST

Under coach Fernando Santos, Portugal's gameplan is pretty straightforward: stay solid, keep a clean sheet and rely on either of their prolific strikers, Cristiano Ronaldo or Andre Silva, to grab a goal at the other end.

It makes perfect sense, then, for the Portuguese to line up in an old-fashioned 4-4-2 which demands that the opposition breaks down two well-drilled banks of four before even getting a sight of Rui Patricio's goal.

In possession, Portugal look to get their creative midfielders, Manchester City's Bernardo Silva and Monaco's Joao Moutinho, on the ball as much as possible, with the aim of supplying the front two quickly. Sporting Lisbon's William Carvalho is the holder in midfield in front of a tightly-organised defence, led by the veteran Pepe, which is quite happy to sit deep and soak up pressure.

It's a functional, not especially attractive style, but it works for Portugal.

PORTUGAL AT THE WORLD CUP

Portugal reached the semi-finals in 2006 before losing out to France

• Portugal didn't appear at the World Cup until 1966, but they made up for lost time by reaching the semi-finals. Up against hosts England at Wembley, the Portuguese gave a good account of themselves before losing 2-1. In the previous round against surprise packages North Korea, Portugal made one of the greatest comebacks at the finals, fighting back from 3-0 down at Goodison Park to win 5-3.

• The brilliant Eusebio, arguably Portugal's greatest ever player, banged in four goals in that game, and with nine goals in total was the tournament's leading scorer.

• Portugal didn't reach the finals again until 1986, and began the tournament with an excellent 1-0 win over England, thanks to a late goal by Carlos Manuel. However, a dispute over prize money undermined the team's collective spirit and after defeats to Poland and Morocco they were knocked out.

• The Portuguese had another long wait before returning to the finals, but finally did so in 2002 with a fine team dubbed the 'Golden Generation'. Sadly for their fans, Luis Figo and co. failed to deliver when it really mattered, losing to both the USA and co-hosts South

Korea between a 4-0 thrashing of Poland that demonstrated what the side was capable of on a good day.

• At the 2006 finals in Germany, Portugal were involved in the dirtiest match in World Cup history against the Netherlands in the last 16. Overworked Russian referee Valentin Ivanov sent off four players and booked 16 in a match that the Portuguese won 1-0. They then beat England on penalties thanks to the heroics of goalkeeper Ricardo, who saved spot-kicks from Frank Lampard, Steven Gerrard and Jamie Carragher. In the semi-finals, though, Portugal lost by a single goal to France.

• In South Africa in 2010 Portugal recorded their biggest ever win at the finals – a 7-0 tonking of minnows North Korea. That victory helped the Portuguese advance to the last 16, where they came up against neighbours Spain. In a hard-fought encounter, a solitary goal by David Villa was enough to see the Spanish through.

• At their last appearance at the finals in 2014 Portugal never really recovered from a 4-0 thrashing by Germany and were eventually pipped to second place in their group on goal difference by the USA.

PREVIOUS TOURNAMENTS

1930 Did not enter	1966 Third place	1994 Did not qualify
1934 Did not qualify	1970 Did not qualify	1998 Did not qualify
1938 Did not qualify	1974 Did not qualify	2002 Round 1
1950 Did not qualify	1978 Did not qualify	2006 Fourth place
1954 Did not qualify	1982 Did not qualify	2010 Round 2
1958 Did not qualify	1986 Round 1	2014 Round 1
1962 Did not qualify	1990 Did not qualify	

SPAIN

After failing to put up much of a defence of their trophy in Brazil in 2014 and then losing their European crown two years ago, Spain have been rejuvenated and head towards Russia on the back of a long unbeaten run. With a squad packed full of wonderfully talented players from La Liga powerhouses Barcelona and Real Madrid, 'La Roja' will once again be a force to be reckoned with this summer.

ESPAÑA vs COSTA RICA
PARTIDO INTERNACIONAL AMISTOSO

Under boss Julen Lopetegui, who took charge after the European Championships, Spain breezed through their qualifying campaign, finishing five points clear of second-placed Italy and conceding just three goals in 10 matches. Their excellent form rather made a mockery of Fifa's decision to demote the Spanish to the second pot of nations for the World Cup draw, although they haven't suffered too much as a result.

> **"Without a doubt we have the toughest group in the World Cup."**
> Spain coach
> Julen Lopetegui

Formerly in charge of the country's Under-19 and Under-21 teams, Lopetegui has freshened up an ageing squad by giving opportunities to a number of exciting younger players, headed by new Real Madrid sensation, 22-year-old attacking midfielder Marco Asensio. Meanwhile, midfielders Isco and Koke, of Real and Atletico Madrid respectively, and Real right-back Dani Carvajal are a promising trio in their mid-twenties who could also figure as starters.

Otherwise, the Spanish team is full of very familiar names from previous tournaments, including veteran midfielders Andres Iniesta, David Silva and Sergio Busquets and central defenders Gerard Pique and captain Sergio Ramos. In goal, of course, there is Manchester United's David de Gea, regarded by most observers as the best in the world in his position, while up front Chelsea's Alvaro Morata and Atletico's Diego Costa will compete for the lone striker's role in a 4-5-1 formation.

Spain's mix of youth and experience looks just about right, and a place in the last four is surely not beyond them.

THE GAFFER
JULEN LOPETEGUI

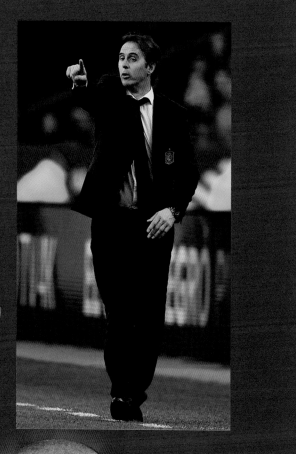

Appointed Spain manager as successor to the long-serving Vicente del Bosque in July 2016, Julen Lopetegui has yet to experience defeat in his new role after 16 matches in charge, including 10 in the qualifying campaign for Russia 2018.

It all adds up to a very satisfying start for the 51-year-old, especially as his credentials for the top job have been widely debated in the Spanish media. Briefly manager of Rayo Vallecano in 2003, Lopetegui then had a spell as a TV sports commentator, before returning to coaching with Castilla, Real Madrid's reserve team. In 2010 he began working for the Spanish FA, and two years later guided the Under-19 team to victory in the European Championships. A year later Lopetegui repeated that success with the Under-21s, who beat Italy 4-2 in the final in Jerusalem. In 2014 he became manager of Porto but failed to deliver any silverware and was unceremoniously sacked halfway through the 2015/16 season.

A proud Basque, Lopetegui was a goalkeeper in his playing days, winning one cap for Spain in 1993 during a 17-year career which saw him briefly turn out for Real Madrid and Barcelona as well as having longer stints with Logrones and Rayo Vallecano.

KEY PLAYER

DAVID SILVA

A supremely talented playmaker who possesses excellent ball control and the ability to thread a killer pass through the most well-organised of defences, David Silva continues to sparkle even at the age of 32.

First capped in 2006, he was an integral figure in the Spanish side that won Euro 2008, beating Germany in the final. Silva was less involved in his country's successful World Cup campaign two years later, but he was back in the fold for Euro 2012, heading the first goal in Spain's 4-0 thrashing of Italy in the final.

Nicknamed 'El Mago' ('The Magician') for his sublime skills on the ball, Silva joined Manchester City from Valencia for £24 million in 2010. He has since enjoyed huge success at the Etihad, helping City win the FA Cup in his first season at the club, two League Cups and the Premier League title in both 2012 and 2014.

ONE TO WATCH
ISCO

Isco has faced stiff competition to establish himself in Spain's midfield, but is now an almost guaranteed name on the teamsheet. After missing out on selection for the 2014 World Cup in Brazil, the Real Madrid star will be looking to stamp his mark on this summer's tournament.

He certainly has the talent to do so. A composed player with an eye for goal – he scored five times during the qualifying campaign – Isco has been compared to Zinedine Zidane by none other than the French legend himself.

Born Francisco Roman Alarcon Suarez, Isco started out with Valencia before moving to Malaga in 2011. The following year his eye-catching performances earned him the Golden Boy award, given to the most impressive footballer in Europe aged under 21. He signed for Real for around £25 million in June 2013 and has since helped the Spanish giants win the Champions League three times.

Isco has played for Spain at every age level from Under-16 upwards, making his senior debut in a 3-1 win against Uruguay in February 2013.

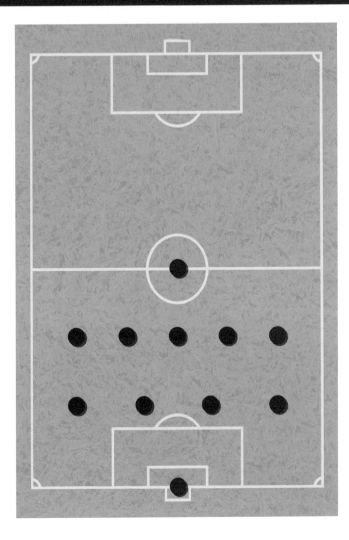

TACTICS BOARD

MIDFIELD DOMINATION

Although he experimented with a strikerless system in the qualifiers, Spain boss Julen Lopetegui is likely to adopt a 4-5-1 formation at the World Cup, with either Chelsea centre forward Alvaro Morata or former Blue Diego Costa at the point of the attack.

As ever, Spain will have a cadre of small, technically gifted midfielders buzzing around their target man, all aiming to keep possession through short, quick passes which move the opposition defence around and create sudden spaces to exploit.

The likes of Andres Iniesta, David Silva and Isco are all masters of this 'tika-taka' style of play, while Sergio Busquets' main role is to win the ball back whenever it's lost.

With two full-backs, probably Barcelona's Jordi Alba and Real Madrid's Dani Carvajal, also pushing into midfield, Spain can easily overwhelm opponents but they need to be careful ageing central defenders Sergio Ramos and Gerard Pique are not exposed to swift counter-attacks.

SPAIN AT THE WORLD CUP

• Spain's first ever World Cup match saw them defeat Brazil 3-1 in 1934. Their next game with hosts Italy went to a replay before the injury-hit Spanish went down to a 1-0 defeat.

• Spain enjoyed better fortune at the 1950 tournament in Brazil, beating the USA, Chile and England to enter the final pool of four teams. After a satisfactory opening 2-2 draw with eventual winners Uruguay, the Spanish were crushed 6-1 by Brazil and 3-1 by Sweden to finish fourth.

It literally rained gold when Spain won the World Cup in 2010

• With Real Madrid dominating the European Cup in the late 1950s and early 1960s, Spain should have been a real force during this era. However, the Spanish made little impression at the World Cup, failing to qualify for the 1958 tournament and going home after the group stages in both 1962 and 1966.

• As hosts in 1982, Spain fared only slightly better. After suffering a humiliating 1-0 defeat by Northern Ireland, the Spanish just scraped into the second round on goals scored. A 2-1 defeat to West Germany pretty much ended their chances of reaching the semi-finals, making their draw with England largely academic.

• Four years later Spain stormed into the quarter-finals thanks to a magnificent 5-1 demolition of Denmark in the Round of 16 in Mexico, with Real Madrid striker Emilio 'The Vulture' Butragueno hitting four of the goals. However, a penalty shoot-out defeat to Belgium in the last eight dashed their World Cup dreams once more.

• Spain also made it to the last eight in 2002 before going down to co-hosts South Korea. Mind you, they were desperately unlucky to have two seemingly valid goals disallowed by the officials.

• Spain's luck finally changed in South Africa in 2010 when they won the competition for the first time. Their campaign began badly with a shock 1-0 defeat to Switzerland, but they recovered to get through the group stage and then saw off Portugal, Paraguay and Germany before meeting the Netherlands in the final in Johannesburg. Refusing to be intimidated by the crudely physical tactics of the Dutch, Spain lifted the trophy thanks to an Andres Iniesta goal deep into extra-time.

• Sadly for their fans, Spain made a calamitous defence of their trophy in 2014, losing 5-1 to the Netherlands and 2-0 to Chile to go out of the competition after just two matches. In their final game, Spain beat Australia 3-0.

PREVIOUS TOURNAMENTS

1930 Did not enter	1966 Round 1	1994 Quarter-finals
1934 Quarter-finals	1970 Did not qualify	1998 Round 1
1938 Withdrew	1974 Did not qualify	2002 Quarter-finals
1950 Fourth place	1978 Round 1	2006 Round 2
1954 Did not qualify	1982 Round 2	2010 Winners
1958 Did not qualify	1986 Quarter-finals	2014 Round 1
1962 Round 1	1990 Round 2	

MOROCCO

The first African nation to appear at the World Cup in the post-war era, Morocco are back at the finals after a 20-year gap. Something of an unknown quantity, the north Africans will go to Russia with enormous confidence in their backline. Incredibly, in six final group qualifying games the Atlas Lions didn't concede a single goal, suggesting that they will be a tough nut for their opponents to crack this summer.

Much of the credit for that defensive meanness must go to head coach Herve Renard, a Frenchman who had previously taken both Zambia (in 2012) and Ivory Coast (in 2015) to glory in the Africa Cup of Nations, making him the first man to win this competition with two different countries. The tactically astute Renard, though, has been fortunate in having one of the continent's best defenders, Juventus' Medhi Benatia, at the heart of his rearguard. His colleagues in the back four, meanwhile, include Wolves' Romain Saiss and a young Real Madrid prodigy, 19-year-old right-back Achraf Hakimi.

> **"It looks difficult on paper but nothing is impossible in football."**
> Morocco coach Herve Renard

In midfield, Renard can call on the talented Ajax playmaker Hakim Ziyech, who previously played at youth levels for the Netherlands before switching allegiance to Morocco in 2015. It will be interesting to see if he also finds a starting position for Southampton's Sofiane Boufal. Very much a maverick, Boufal demonstrated his undoubted ability with one of the goals of the 2017/18 Premier League season, a mazy run past six West Brom defenders before he calmly slotted the ball into the corner of the net – but such memorable moments have been all too rare in a stop-start career.

For all their defensive solidity, Morocco are likely to be hampered by their lack of a prolific striker – Khalid Boutaib of Turkish outfit Yeni Malatyaspor is most likely to lead the line – and it is difficult to see them progressing out of a tough group.

MOROCCO AT THE WORLD CUP

• In 1970 Morocco became the first African country since Egypt in 1934 to compete at the World Cup. They shocked West Germany by taking the lead in their opening game before going down to a 2-1 defeat, and they went home with a point from their last match against Bulgaria.

• Back in Mexico again for the 1986 tournament, Morocco surprisingly topped their group after drawing 0-0 with both Poland and England and then beating Portugal 3-1. They proved sturdy opponents, too, for West Germany in the last 16 before succumbing to a late goal.

• Eight years later Morocco fared less well, losing to Belgium, Saudi Arabia and the Netherlands to finish bottom of their group.

• At their last appearance in the finals at France in 1998 Morocco were desperately unlucky not to reach the knockout phase. A 3-0 hammering of Scotland appeared to have booked their berth, but then news came through that Norway had somehow pipped them to second place with a shock 2-1 victory over reigning world champions Brazil.

PREVIOUS TOURNAMENTS

1930 Did not enter	1966 Withdrew	1994 Round 1
1934 Did not enter	1970 Round 1	1998 Round 1
1938 Did not enter	1974 Did not qualify	2002 Did not qualify
1950 Did not enter	1978 Did not qualify	2006 Did not qualify
1954 Did not enter	1982 Did not qualify	2010 Did not qualify
1958 Did not enter	1986 Round 2	2014 Did not qualify
1962 Did not qualify	1990 Did not qualify	

KEY PLAYER

MEDHI BENATIA

The backbone of the Morocco defence which didn't concede a single goal in six qualifying matches against Ivory Coast, Gabon and Mali, Medhi Benatia is a tall, strong and athletic centre-back who tackles hard and is dominant in the air.

Born and raised in France by an Algerian mother and a Moroccan father, Benatia began his career with Marseille but after a couple of loan spells he moved on to Clermont. A switch to Italian side Udinese in 2010 saw him progress further and in 2013 he joined Roma, where he was voted into the Serie A Team of the Year after helping the Lupi finish second behind champions Juventus. In 2014 Benatia was signed by Bayern Munich for around £20 million and although he never quite held down a regular first-team place he did win two Bundesliga titles with the German giants before joining Juventus on loan, a move which became permanent in 2017.

Now aged 30, Benatia is his country's captain and one of Morocco's most experienced players with more than 50 caps to his name.

IRAN

For the first time in their history Iran will be playing at consecutive World Cups, having also featured at the previous finals in Brazil. Manager Carlos Queiroz, who was appointed to the role in 2011 after spells in charge of Real Madrid and Portugal, deserves much of the credit for that achievement and his vast experience will be invaluable to a squad hoping to make a first appearance in the knockout phase.

Queiroz's men head to Russia on the back of outstanding form in the qualifiers, which saw them remain undefeated in 18 matches in total and, incredibly, keep clean sheets in 12 straight games – a superb run which enabled the Iranians to become the second country to book their place in the finals, securing automatic qualification with a comfortable 2-0 home win against Uzbekistan.

> **"The most important thing is to play with ambition and leave the World Cup honorably."**
> Iran coach
> Carlos Queiroz

Unsurprisingly given these statistics, Iran's main strength lies in their defensive structure and organisation. Goalkeeper Ali Beiranvand of Tehran giants Persepolis is an influential figure, possessing a huge throw which he uses to good effect to launch counter-attacks, while his club-mate Jalal Hosseini, an experienced centre-back with over 100 caps, is the mainstay of the back four.

In midfield, Iran look to Ashkan Dejagah, a former German Under-21 international who had a stint with Fulham a few years ago, for inspiration and creativity. Dejagah now wears his country's armband after former skipper Masoud Shojaei was banned from representing his country for life after playing for his club side, Greek outfit Panionios, in a Europa League tie against Maccabi Tel Aviv in violation of an Iranian government decree that its sportsmen should not compete against Israelis. An experienced and talented midfielder, Shojaei will be a big miss for Iran at the finals.

Up front, Iran rely heavily on star player Sadar Azmoun, but he will need support if 'Team Melli', as they are known, are to make it out of a tough group.

IRAN AT THE WORLD CUP

• Iran made their World Cup debut in 1978, pulling off a major surprise when they drew 1-1 with Scotland. That result, however, was sandwiched between heavy defeats against the Netherlands (0-3) and Peru (1-4).

• At France '98, Iran followed a 1-0 loss to Yugoslavia with a 2-1 victory over the USA – 'The Great Satan' according to Iran's government – which prompted scenes of jubilation back in Tehran. Even the subsequent 2-0 loss to Germany could not poop the national party atmosphere.

• Sadly for their fans, Iran failed to reproduce those heroics at the 2006 finals, losing 3-1 to Mexico and 2-0 to Portugal before salvaging some pride with a 1-1 draw against Angola.

• On their last appearance at the finals in 2014 Iran recorded their first ever World Cup clean sheet in a 0-0 draw with Nigeria. They nearly repeated that scoreline against Argentina before they were undone by a late piece of Lionel Messi magic, and their tournament ended on a low note with a disappointing 3-1 defeat to Bosnia and Herzegovina.

PREVIOUS TOURNAMENTS

1930 Did not enter	1966 Did not enter	1994 Did not qualify
1934 Did not enter	1970 Did not enter	1998 Round 1
1938 Did not enter	1974 Did not qualify	2002 Did not qualify
1950 Did not enter	1978 Round 1	2006 Round 1
1954 Did not enter	1982 Withdrew	2010 Did not qualify
1958 Did not enter	1986 Disqualified	2014 Round 1
1962 Did not enter	1990 Did not qualify	

KEY PLAYER

SARDAR AZMOUN

A striker who has been compared to Zlatan Ibrahimovic for his heading ability and prowess in the penalty box, Sardar Azmoun is already Iran's fifth top goalscorer ever at the tender age of 23. No wonder, then, that the Russia-based forward is on the radar of numerous European clubs, and has been linked with Arsenal, Everton and Liverpool.

Azmoun started out with Sepahan, the leading Iranian club, where his prolific form in the youth team quickly attracted the attention of foreign scouts. He moved to Rubin Kazan aged 17, becoming the first Iranian to play in the Russian Premier League, but only really got into his stride after a messy transfer to FC Rostov.

After helping his new club reach the Champions League proper he became the first Iranian for 11 years to score in the group stage in a 2-1 defeat against Atletico Madrid in November 2016 and was also on the scoresheet in a famous 3-2 win against Bayern Munich. In July 2017, following a protracted dispute about which club owned him, he returned from Rostov to Rubin Kazan.

FRANCE

Winners of the World Cup in 1998 when they hosted the tournament, France will be one of the favourites to lift the trophy again this summer. Much will depend, though, on whether Les Bleus have recovered from the psychological scars left by their shattering defeat in the final of the 2016 European Championships, when they were beaten by underdogs Portugal at the Stade de France.

The answer to that question was not fully provided by France's qualifying campaign. At times, coach Didier Deschamps' young, vibrant side were superb, notably in a 4-0 annihilation of the Netherlands, but they also struggled at various points, drawing with both Belarus and Luxembourg and losing in Sweden. On the face of it, such inconsistency does not bode well for the finals, where one bad game can spell the end.

> **"France will go to this World Cup in Russia with lots of ambition."**
> France coach
> Didier Deschamps

Yet, France have such an impressive squad, packed full of fantastic players, that they must be considered genuine contenders. Quality runs through whatever team Deschamps puts out, from goalkeeper Hugo Lloris, through central defenders Raphael Varane and Laurent Koscielny, to midfield powerhouses Paul Pogba and N'Golo Kante. Up front, meanwhile, Les Bleus have a range of options which other countries can only dream about. Arsenal's Olivier Giroud and Atletico Madrid's Antoine Griezmann are the favoured starters in Deschamps' preferred 4-4-2 formation, leaving the likes of the Gunners' Alexandre Lacazette, Manchester United's Anthony Martial and PSG wonderkid Kylian Mbappe fighting between them to even make an impact from the bench.

There is a sense that Les Bleus, given all the talent at their disposal, have yet to fulfil their true potential and as a team don't yet match the sum of their parts. If Deschamps can solve that conundrum, though, the French could go far in the tournament – even all the way to the final.

THE GAFFER
DIDIER DESCHAMPS

Appointed manager of France in July 2012, Didier Deschamps is now the third-longest post-war boss of Les Bleus. He has enjoyed reasonable success in his time in the hotseat, taking his country to the quarter-finals of the 2014 World Cup in Brazil and the final of the 2016 European Championships, when France surprisingly lost 1-0 to Portugal on home soil.

Deschamps began his managerial career with Monaco, who he guided to the Champions League final in 2004. After a short spell with Juventus, he returned to France with Marseille, leading them to a first French league title for 18 years in 2010.

However, Deschamps is best known in his native country as the captain of the France side which won the World Cup as hosts in 1998, and two years later claimed the European Championships. He retired from international football shortly after that second triumph, having accumulated a then French record 103 caps.

An intelligent ball-playing defensive midfielder who was once scornfully dismissed as a mere "water carrier" by maverick French striker Eric Cantona, Deschamps also won a sackful of silverware at club level, including the Champions League with both Marseille and Juventus and the FA Cup with Chelsea in 2000.

KEY PLAYER

PAUL POGBA

A hard-running, all-action midfielder whose long legs eat up the ground when he goes on one of his trademark rampaging forward bursts, Paul Pogba has established himself as the most influential player in France's star-studded midfield.

Now 24, he made his debut for Les Bleus in 2013 and the following year was named the Best Young Player at the World Cup in Brazil. In 2016 he was part of the French team that were runners-up in the European Championships.

At club level, Pogba won four successive Scudetto titles with Juventus, before becoming the world's most expensive footballer at the time when he rejoined Manchester United, the club he had initially signed for as a 16-year-old from Le Havre, for £89.3 million in August 2016. He paid back some of that hefty fee by helping United win the League Cup and Europa League in his first season back at Old Trafford.

ONE TO WATCH
KYLIAN MBAPPE

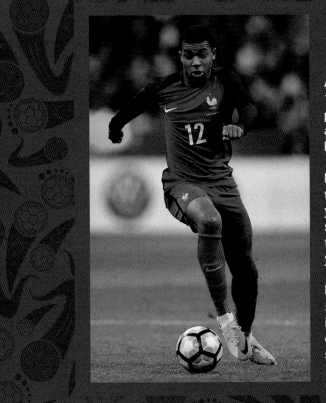

Although he only made his debut for France in March 2017, 19-year-old Kylian Mbappe could be one of the outstanding performers at this summer's World Cup. Fast, strong, direct and skilful, the Paris Saint-Germain striker has everything in his locker to become a genuine star of the global game.

A product of the famous Clairefontaine academy, Mbappe has already achieved a lot in his fledgling career. He holds the records for Monaco as the club's youngest player and youngest goalscorer – in both cases beating past benchmarks set by the legendary Thierry Henry – and in 2017 helped the team from the French Riviera win their first league title for 17 years, contributing an impressive 26 goals in all competitions.

In the summer of 2017 he moved to PSG, initially on loan, but for an agreed future transfer fee reported to be around £166 million, making him the second most expensive player in the world behind his teammate Neymar. That staggering deal means the eyes of the world will be on him in Russia, but such is his talent Mbappe could yet surpass all expectations.

TACTICS BOARD

STRONG SPINE

Although he can easily adapt Les Bleus to a 4-3-3 system, France coach Didier Deschamps is most likely to send out his team in a 4-4-2 formation, with strikers Antoine Griezmann and Olivier Giroud leading the attack.

It's a tactical approach which has been lambasted by the critics as being unsubtle, basic, easy to counter and risky, with the possibility of France being outnumbered in midfield. This, though, is an area where Les Bleus are exceptionally strong and powerful, thanks to the presence in the centre of Paul Pogba and N'Golo Kante. This pair will look to feed the ball out wide whenever possible, where Deschamps has numerous exciting options including the likes of Anthony Martial, Bayern Munich's Kingsley Coman and Monaco's Thomas Lemar.

At the back, meanwhile, Laurent Koscielny and Raphael Varane are a pacy central pair who can cover for the forward advances of attacking full-backs Djibril Sidibe and Lucas Digne.

FRANCE AT THE WORLD CUP

The legendary Zinedine Zidane inspired France's 1998 World Cup triumph

• France played in the first ever World Cup match, thrashing Mexico 4-1 in Montevideo, Uruguay, on 13 July 1930. In front of a paltry crowd in the Pocitos stadium, France's Lucien Laurent wrote himself into World Cup history by scoring the tournament's first ever goal after 19 minutes.

• **France hosted the tournament for the first time in 1938, and the hosts got off to a dream start when they scored after just 40 seconds in the first round against neighbours Belgium. In the quarter-finals, though, they came up against the holders Italy and went down to a 3-1 defeat.**

• In Sweden in 1958 France fared better, finishing in third place after losing 5-2 to eventual champions Brazil in the semi-finals. French striker Just Fontaine set a still unbeaten record for the tournament by scoring 13 goals, including three against Paraguay and four in the play-off for third place against West Germany.

• **In 1982 France reached the semi-finals again, but lost in the first World Cup penalty shoot-out** against West Germany. The game, though, is best remembered for a violent challenge by German goalkeeper Harald Schumacher on Patrick Battiston, which knocked out three of the Frenchman's teeth and left him unconscious. Incredibly, the referee didn't even award France a free-kick.

• After a third semi-final defeat in 1986, France finally reached the final on home soil in 1998.

Their opponents, reigning champions Brazil, were beaten surprisingly easily, star player Zinedine Zidane scoring twice and Arsenal midfielder Emmanuel Petit adding a third as France won 3-0. More than a million people celebrated their country's triumph in the streets of Paris.

• **Four years later France put up an unexpectedly weak defence of their trophy, going out in the group phase after shock defeats to Senegal and Denmark.**

• Les Bleus returned to form in 2006, reaching the final in Germany where they lost on penalties to Italy. Sadly for his many admirers, the brilliant career of midfield maestro Zinedine Zidane ended on a low note as he was sent off for headbutting Italian defender Marco Materazzi.

• **After a chaotic campaign in 2010 during which the French players briefly went on strike, Les Bleus performed much better in Brazil four years later, reaching the quarter-finals where they lost 1-0 to eventual winners Germany.**

PREVIOUS TOURNAMENTS

1930 Round 1	1966 Round 1	1994 Did not qualify
1934 Round 1	1970 Did not qualify	1998 Winners
1938 Quarter-finals	1974 Did not qualify	2002 Round 1
1950 Withdrew	1978 Round 1	2006 Runners-up
1954 Round 1	1982 Fourth place	2010 Round 1
1958 Third place	1986 Third place	2014 Quarter-finals
1962 Did not qualify	1990 Did not qualify	

AUSTRALIA

Australia will be appearing at their fourth consecutive World Cup, and can now count themselves as tournament regulars – not bad for a country which only appeared at one other tournament before 2006. However, the Aussies' preparations for the finals were thrown into turmoil when their manager, Ange Postecoglou, resigned just days after seeing his team clinch their place in Russia, citing the toll the job had taken on him.

Almost certainly the Aussies' marathon qualifying campaign had something to do with Postecoglou's shock decision. The Socceroos played 22 games in total, being forced into two-legged play-offs with both Syria and Honduras after being pipped by Saudi Arabia for automatic qualification on goal difference. The fact that the Aussies successfully battled their way through such a convoluted fixture list was testament to their resilience and determination – qualities that will serve them well this summer.

> **"Any team you get at this stage is going to be tough but I fancy us to go through."**
> Australia midfielder Massimo Luongo

As in the past when the Socceroos could call on the talents of stars like Harry Kewell and Mark Viduka,

British-based players form the backbone of the current Australian team. Brighton's Matthew Ryan is a reliable presence in goal, while Bristol City's Bailey Wright is one of three centre-backs in the Aussies' usual 3-4-3 system. In midfield, skipper Mile Jedinak, now with Aston Villa after five years at Crystal Palace, plays the holding role and has a good relationship with the more creative Tom Rogic of Celtic.

In attack, Australia are heavily reliant on the evergreen Tim Cahill, still banging in the goals – including an impressive 11 in qualification – at the ripe old age of 38. A superb header of the ball, he will look to the wide players, who might well be Huddersfield's Aaron Mooy and Hull's Jackson Irvine, to supply him with a steady stream of high crosses.

Overall, though, Australia look short on quality and a first-round exit appears likely.

AUSTRALIA AT THE WORLD CUP

• Australia first appeared on the world stage in 1974 in West Germany, but returned Down Under without managing to score a single goal in their three group games. However, the Socceroos did at least gain a point from a 0-0 draw with Chile.

• The Aussies had to wait until 2006 before reaching the finals again, and did their country proud by battling through the group stage thanks to a late equaliser from gifted winger Harry Kewell in an exciting 2-2 draw with Croatia. Superbly organised by Dutch boss Guus Hiddink, the Socceroos then gave eventual winners Italy an almighty scare before falling to a controversial last-minute penalty, which was converted by striker Francesco Totti.

• Four years later Australia came close to reaching the last 16 again but were just beaten by Ghana to second place in their group on goal difference.

• The Socceroos, though, performed poorly on their last World Cup outing in Brazil in 2014, losing their group games against Chile, the Netherlands and Spain and conceding nine goals in the process.

PREVIOUS TOURNAMENTS

1930 Did not enter	1966 Did not qualify	1994 Did not qualify
1934 Did not enter	1970 Did not qualify	1998 Did not qualify
1938 Did not enter	1974 Round 1	2002 Did not qualify
1950 Did not enter	1978 Did not qualify	2006 Round 2
1954 Did not enter	1982 Did not qualify	2010 Round 1
1958 Did not enter	1986 Did not qualify	2014 Round 1
1962 Did not enter	1990 Did not qualify	

KEY PLAYER

MILE JEDINAK

A rugged, tough-tackling defensive midfielder, Australia captain Mile Jedinak delivered an inspirational performance in his country's World Cup qualification play-off with Honduras, scoring a hat-trick (including two penalties) in the second leg to secure the Socceroos' place at the finals in Russia.

Although the 33-year-old is highly unlikely to lift the trophy in Moscow on 15 July he already has some impressive international silverware to his name, having skippered the Aussies in the final of the 2015 Asian Cup, which saw them defeat South Korea 2-1 after extra-time.

Asian International Footballer of the Year in 2014 and the owner of more than 70 caps, the curly-haired Jedinak began his club career with Australian outfits Sydney United and Central Coast Mariners. A spell in Turkey with Genclerbirligi followed before he pitched up at Crystal Palace in 2011, helping the Eagles reach the Premier League via the play-offs two years later after a 1-0 win against Watford at Wembley. After five years at Selhurst Park, where he became a cult figure with Palace fans, he joined Aston Villa in the summer of 2016.

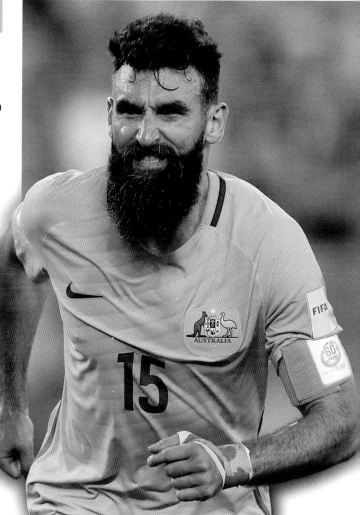

67

PERU

Peru are appearing at their first World Cup for 36 years, having last featured at the finals in Spain in 1982. The South Americans left their fans biting their fingernails to the very end before their qualification was secured, and were the last nation to book their place in Russia thanks to a 2-0 aggregate play-off victory over New Zealand.

While their supporters are thrilled to be finally back on the world stage, there is no doubt that Peru are rather fortunate to be going to this summer's football party. Fighting with Chile for the all-important fifth place in the South American qualifying section, the Peruvians were indebted to a late own goal by Colombia goalkeeper David Ospina which gained them the point they needed to edge out their neighbours on goal difference. Earlier in the campaign, meanwhile, Peru's 2-0 defeat away to Bolivia was scratched by Fifa and turned into a very welcome – and, as it turned out, absolutely crucial – 3-0 win after the home side fielded an ineligible player.

> **"It's an interesting group with very good teams. I think it suits us."**
> Peru coach
> Ricardo Gareca

Still, under Argentinian coach Ricardo Gareca, Peru are an improving side who play attractive football in a fluid 4-2-3-1 formation, and they have the talent to compete for a place in the knockout stage.

Since taking his side to third place at the Copa America in 2015, Gareca has introduced a number of younger players to the squad, but the side's core remains centred around three veterans: captain and defensive leader Alberto Rodriguez, fellow centre-back Christian Ramos and speedy Lokomotiv Moscow wideman Jefferson Farfan. This trio's different talents are complemented by Sao Paulo's Christian Cueva, a creative midfielder who possesses the ability to unlock the tightest of defences with a pinpoint pass.

However, Peru will miss star striker Paolo Guerrero, who is currently serving a lengthy ban having failed a drugs test in October 2017.

PERU AT THE WORLD CUP

• Peru competed at the first World Cup in 1930, but failed to impress in defeats to Romania and hosts and eventual champions Uruguay.

• **The South Americans did much better on their next appearance in 1970 in Mexico, reaching the quarter-finals where they lost an entertaining match 4-2 to eventual winners Brazil. Peru's star was striker Teofilo Cubillas, who** was awarded the Fifa World Cup Young Player award after coming third in the scoring charts behind West German hotshot Gerd Muller and Brazilian legend Jairzinho with five goals.

• In 1978 Peru again made it out of their group after beating Scotland (3-1) and Iran (4-1) and registering a creditable draw with the Netherlands. However, the Peruvians' form completely deserted them in the second group stage and they ended up bottom of the pile after defeats to Brazil, Poland and hosts Argentina.

• On their last appearance at the finals in 1982 in Spain, Peru began with encouraging draws against Cameroon and Italy before a 5-1 hammering at the hands of Poland brought their tournament to a shuddering halt.

PREVIOUS TOURNAMENTS

1930 Round 1	1966 Did not qualify	1994 Did not qualify
1934 Withdrew	1970 Quarter-finals	1998 Did not qualify
1938 Did not enter	1974 Did not qualify	2002 Did not qualify
1950 Withdrew	1978 Round 2	2006 Did not qualify
1954 Withdrew	1982 Round 1	2010 Did not qualify
1958 Did not qualify	1986 Did not qualify	2014 Did not qualify
1962 Did not qualify	1990 Did not qualify	

KEY PLAYER

JEFFERSON FARFAN

In the absence of their all-time top scorer Paolo Guerrero, who is serving a 12-month ban after failing a drugs test, Peru will look for goals from pacy forward Jefferson Farfan.

The playing conditions and atmosphere in the stadiums will be familiar to the 33-year-old as he is now plying his trade in Russia with Lokomotiv Moscow. Earlier in his career, he enjoyed great success with PSV, winning four league titles with the Dutch giants, before moving to Schalke, with whom he won the German Cup in 2011.

Since making his debut for Peru in 2003, Farfan has notched 23 goals for his country, the most important of which helped the South Americans overcome New Zealand in the intercontinental play-off that decided the last of the finalists for this summer's tournament. However, he has also experienced some low moments with the national team – none more so than in 2007 when he was one of several Peruvian players to be banned for three months when they were spotted in a nightclub a couple of days before a World Cup qualifier.

DENMARK

Denmark will only be appearing at their fifth World Cup this summer, but have a decent record in past tournaments. Although they failed to get out of their group at their last finals in 2010, the Danes made it through to the knockout stages on the other three occasions and will expect to do so again after being drawn in a group that does not look especially demanding.

The Danes will also be bouyed by their recent excellent form, which is in marked contrast to how they started the qualification process. However, to the relief of their fans, their results picked up and they eventually finished second behind group winners Poland. Drawn against the Republic of Ireland in the play-offs, the Danes were held to a 0-0 draw in Copenhagen but outclassed their opponents in the return leg, star player Christian Eriksen scoring a stunning hat-trick in a crushing 5-1 victory.

The Tottenham midfielder is at the heart of all Denmark's best moves, and is well-supported by Copenhagen's William Kvist and Werder Bremen's Thomas Delaney. Behind this trio, the Danes possess a solid defence which includes captain Simon Kjaer of Sevilla and Chelsea's Andreas Christensen, an unflappable centre-back with superb positional sense. In goal, meanwhile, Leicester's Kasper Schmeichel is fast becoming one of the best in the world in his position, and is capable of making match-winning saves.

At the other end of the pitch, though, Denmark have problems. Experienced manager Age Hareide can call on a number of strikers, including former Arsenal forward Nicklas Bendtner, Feyenoord's Nicolai Jorgensen and one-time Cardiff flop Andreas Cornelius, but none of them really cut the mustard in qualifying. Unless they can find a cutting edge to complement Eriksen's sublime midfield skills it's difficult to see the Danes progressing beyond the last 16.

> **"It's a very interesting group spread all over the world, playing teams we don't play that much."**
>
> Denmark coach
> Age Hareide

DENMARK AT THE WORLD CUP

• An exciting Denmark team, featuring the iconic midfielder Michael Laudrup, performed well at their first ever finals in 1986, beating Scotland, Uruguay and West Germany in the group stage before losing 5-1 to Spain in the last 16.

• The Danes went one better at their next World Cup in France in 1998, reaching the quarter-finals after thrashing Nigeria 4-1 in the last 16. However, despite playing well against Brazil, they had to pack their bags following a 3-2 defeat against the eventual runners-up.

• Denmark again got through the group stages in 2002, thanks partly to victory over reigning champions France. In the last 16, the Danes faced England but were comfortably beaten after Rio Ferdinand, Michael Owen and Emile Heskey all got on the scoresheet in a 3-0 win for the Three Lions.

• Denmark failed to reach the last 16 at their last appearance in the finals in 2010. Although the Danes came from behind to beat Cameroon, that victory was sandwiched between losses to the Netherlands and Japan.

PREVIOUS TOURNAMENTS

1930 Did not enter	1966 Did not qualify	1994 Did not qualify
1934 Did not enter	1970 Did not qualify	1998 Quarter-finals
1938 Did not enter	1974 Did not qualify	2002 Round 2
1950 Did not enter	1978 Did not qualify	2006 Did not qualify
1954 Did not enter	1982 Did not qualify	2010 Round 1
1958 Did not qualify	1986 Round 2	2014 Did not qualify
1962 Did not enter	1990 Did not qualify	

KEY PLAYER

CHRISTIAN ERIKSEN

If Denmark have one player to thank for reaching the World Cup finals in Russia then it's Christian Eriksen. The Tottenham midfielder was on fire throughout the qualification process, contributing an impressive 11 goals – a tally which included a magnificent hat-trick in the Danes' 5-1 thrashing of the Republic of Ireland in the second leg of the teams' play-off in Dublin.

An elegant and creative player who is a potent threat at set pieces, Eriksen moved from Odense Boldklub to Ajax when he was just 16. He soon cemented a place with the Dutch giants, helping them win three league titles before signing for Spurs in 2013 for £13 million.

When he made his international debut in March 2010 against Austria, aged 18, Eriksen became the fourth youngest Danish player ever to appear for the national team. Later that year he was the youngest player to feature at the World Cup in South Africa. Now 26, Eriksen is the only player to be named Danish Footballer of the Year three years running, collecting the award in 2014, 2015 and 2016.

ARGENTINA

Winners of the World Cup in 1978 and 1986, Argentina have also been runners-up three times, most recently last time out in Brazil. With the great Lionel Messi in their ranks, the South Americans will always be mentioned in any discussion of possible champions in Russia, but their recent form has been patchy at best and their qualification campaign was distinctly unimpressive.

Indeed, Argentina's travails in the CONMEBOL section were so bad that the nation went through two managers, Gerardo Martino and Edgardo Bauza, before Jorge Sampaoli finally stepped into the breach and guided 'La Albiceleste' over the line. The former Chile boss was, almost inevitably, indebted to the talismanic Messi for securing Argentina's place in the finals, the Barcelona maestro scoring a magnificent hat-trick in a crucial 3-1 win in Ecuador in the final round of fixtures. That game aside, the Argentinians had problems finding the net in qualifying, managing just 19 in 18 matches – a paltry return for a country boasting the attacking talents of the likes of Sergio Aguero and Gonzalo Higuain in addition to, arguably, the world's best player.

> **"The only thing I can tell our fans is that we will make Argentina proud."**
>
> Argentina coach
> Jorge Sampaoli

If goals are a problem, the South Americans also have concerns at the other end of the pitch. Goalkeeper Sergio Romero, David de Gea's deputy at Manchester United, is steady enough, but the back three in Sampaoli's preferred 3-4-3 formation is distinctly creaky, and was shown to be lacking in pace in a shock 4-2 friendly defeat by group opponents Nigeria in November 2017. There are question marks, too, about the defensive qualities of wing-backs Angel Di Maria and Eduardo Salvio, who normally operate as wingers for their respective clubs, Paris Saint-Germain and Benfica.

The portents, then, are not great for Argentina but only a fool would rule out a team containing the magical Messi.

THE GAFFER
JORGE SAMPAOLI

Appointed as manager of Argentina in May 2017 following the sacking of his predecessor Edgardo Bauza, Jorge Sampaoli led the two-time world champions to the finals in Russia in the remaining qualifiers thanks to three scratchy draws and a Lionel Messi-inspired victory in Ecuador.

Since taking over in the hotseat, the 57-year-old Sampaoli has attempted to change Argentina's style, adopting the high-intensity pressing game made famous by his mentor Marcelo Bielsa. To date the jury is out on the success of this strategy, with critics arguing that Sampaoli doesn't have the young, super-fit players required to make it work effectively.

However, Sampaoli certainly has an impressive CV. After spells with clubs in Peru and Ecuador, he made his name with Universidad de Chile, who he guided to three league titles and the 2011 Copa Sudamericana – the South American equivalent of the Europa League. Then, in a three-year spell as Chile boss he led his side to their first Copa America title following a shoot-out victory over his native Argentina in 2015.

Most recently, Sampaoli was in charge of Sevilla, taking the Andalusian outfit to fourth place in La Liga in 2016 and a place in the Champions League.

KEY PLAYER

SERGIO AGUERO

After struggling for goals during the qualifying campaign, Argentina will be absolutely desperate to have Sergio Aguero fit and firing once the finals start. The Manchester City star is his country's third highest goalscorer of all time and his ability to convert half chances will be vital to the South Americans' chances of success in Russia.

Known as 'El Kun' because of his resemblance to a Japanese cartoon character, Aguero started out with Avellaneda-based giants Independiente before moving to Atletico Madrid with whom he won the inaugural Europa League in 2010. The following year he joined Manchester City for £38 million and in his first season scored 23 Premier League goals, including a dramatic title-clinching winner against QPR on the final day of the season. He is now City's all-time top scorer with more than 180 goals.

First capped in 2006, Aguero helped Argentina win gold at the 2008 Olympics in Beijing.

ONE TO WATCH
PAULO DYBALA

If Juventus striker Paulo Dybala can transfer his club form to international football then he will make a huge impact at this summer's World Cup. Sadly for the 24-year-old he has so far been a disappointment in his limited outings in his country's colours, having collected more red cards than goals.

Still, there is no doubt that the Serie A hitman boasts huge potential. Lively and versatile, he was Juve's top scorer across all competitions in his first season with the club in 2015/16 following his £28 million transfer from Palermo. The next season he successfully played in a deeper role behind new signing Gonzalo Higuain, a fellow Argentinian.

Born in Cordoba to a family with roots in both Poland and Italy, Dybala began his career with local outfit Instituto, becoming the club's youngest ever scorer when he passed the previous benchmark set by the legendary Mario Kempes. The great Argentinian famously scored the goals that won his country the World Cup in 1978; Dybla will dream of doing the same, but first he must find his feet at international level.

TACTICS BOARD

MAXIMUM MESSI

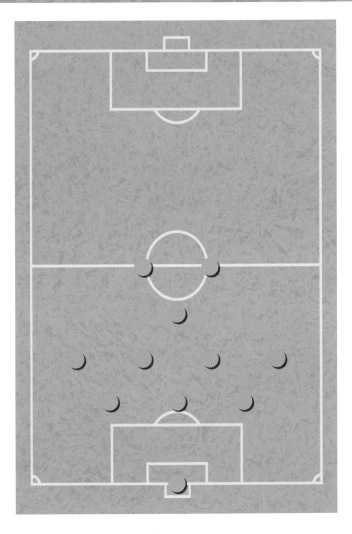

Argentina coach Jorge Sampaoli is known for setting up his teams in unconventional fashion, even experimenting with a bizarre 2-3-5 formation in a recent friendly against Singapore. In Russia, though, he is most likely to adopt a tried and trusted 3-4-3 system, giving star player Lionel Messi maximum leeway to influence the play.

The Barcelona icon will be deployed just behind two strikers, most likely Sergio Aguero and one or other of the Juventus pair of Gonzalo Higuain and Paulo Dybala. Getting Messi on the ball will be crucial, and a prime objective of central midfielders Lucas Biglia and Enzo Perez, of AC Milan and River Plate respectively.

The wide players, Paris Saint-Germain's Angel Di Maria and Benfica's Eduardo Salvio, are far happier going forward than tracking back, which could put a strain on Argentina's ageing three-man defence, marshalled by ball-playing sweeper Javier Mascherano, a colleague of Messi's at Barcelona.

ARGENTINA AT THE WORLD CUP

• Argentina played in the first ever World Cup final, losing 4-2 to neighbours Uruguay in Montevideo. The result didn't go down well in Buenos Aires, where an angry crowd threw stones at the Uruguayan consulate until they were dispersed by gun-wielding police.

• **After crashing out in the first round in 1934 and a subsequent 24-year absence from the tournament, Argentina returned to the finals in 1958 but a tactically inept side were thrashed 6-1 by Czechoslovakia and finished bottom of their group. As if that wasn't bad enough, the players were pelted with coins and vegetables by angry fans on their return from Sweden.**

• At the 1966 tournament in England, Argentina were involved in one of the most notorious matches in World Cup history. Playing the hosts at Wembley in the quarter-finals, Argentina captain Antonio Rattin was sent off in the first half, but initially refused to leave the pitch. After an extremely physical match, which Argentina lost 1-0, England manager Alf Ramsey called the South Americans "animals".

Argentina captain Diego Maradona holds aloft the World Cup trophy in 1986

• **Argentina hosted the tournament in 1978 and thrilled their fanatical fans by reaching the final, where they beat the Netherlands 3-1. Long-haired striker Mario Kempes was the hero of the hour, scoring two of his side's goals as they won in extra-time.**

• Argentina won the tournament for a second time in 1986, thanks mainly to their inspirational captain Diego Maradona. In the quarter-final against England Maradona scored two goals, one a brilliant solo effort and the other punched in with his fist – although he later cheekily claimed that it was scored with the "Hand of God". He banged in another brace in the semi-final against Belgium and then set up Jorge Burruchaga for the winner against West Germany in the final.

• **Four years later Argentina reached the final again in Italy, but were beaten 1-0 by West Germany. In the 65th minute Argentina's Pedro Monzon became the first player to be sent off in the World Cup final and was followed by Gustavo Dezotti, who received a red card in the dying minutes.**

• Eliminated by Germany at the quarter-final stage in both 2006 and 2010, Argentina met their old rivals again in the final in Rio de Janeiro in 2014. Having struggled to perform at their best throughout the tournament, it was no surprise that the Argentinians lost again, going down 1-0 after extra-time.

PREVIOUS TOURNAMENTS

1930 Runners-up	1966 Quarter-finals	1994 Round 2
1934 Round 1	1970 Did not qualify	1998 Quarter-finals
1938 Withdrew	1974 Round 2	2002 Round 1
1950 Withdrew	1978 Winners	2006 Quarter-finals
1954 Withdrew	1982 Round 2	2010 Quarter-finals
1958 Round 1	1986 Winners	2014 Runners-up
1962 Round 1	1990 Runners-up	

ICELAND

With a population of just over 330,000, World Cup debutants Iceland are the smallest nation ever to feature at the finals. However, they will not be going to Russia just to make up the numbers. As they showed at Euro 2016 – when they famously knocked out England – Iceland are a match for anybody on their day and the gritty giant-killers will fancy their chances of causing another upset this summer.

Managed by Heimir Hallgrimsson, a qualified dentist who took sole charge of the team when joint-boss Lars Lagerback stood down after the European Championships, Iceland performed remarkably well in the qualifiers. Drawn in a tough group which included Croatia, Ukraine and Turkey, they ended up topping the table two points clear of the second-placed Croats. That feat was all more praiseworthy considering that Iceland were missing their main striker, Kolbeinn Sigthorsson, through injury for the duration of the campaign.

In his absence, Augsburg's Alfred Finnbogason deputised and chipped in with some valuable goals in the qualifiers. Iceland's main scoring threat, however, comes from Everton's Gylfi Sigurdsson, who can either play up front in Hallgrimsson's preferred 4-4-2 system or drop deeper in a more defensive 4-5-1.

However they line up, Iceland are a hard-working, resilient outfit, whose fighting spirit is epitomised by bearded captain and long-throw specialist Aron Gunnarsson. The Cardiff player is usually accompanied in central midfield by Birkir Bjarnason, a long-haired tussler who joined Aston Villa in 2017. The English connection continues on the right wing with Burnley's Johann Berg Gudmundsson, a left-footer who loves to cut inside and fire off a powerful shot.

In defence, Bristol City's Hordur Magnusson is the central figure and poses a huge threat at set-pieces, as he demonstrated in qualifying with a vital late headed winner against Croatia in June 2017.

> **"It's a little bit of a romantic feeling to play Argentina in the first game."**
>
> Iceland coach
> Heimir Hallgrimsson

ICELAND AT THE WORLD CUP

• Iceland have never appeared at the World Cup before, and didn't enter the qualifying stage until 1958. That proved to be a miserable experience as the island nation was walloped 8-0 by France in their first match, and 8-3 by Belgium three days later.

• Another 16 years passed before Iceland bothered to enter the competition again, but their fortunes didn't improve in the 1974 qualifiers. Predictably, Iceland finished bottom of a group also containing Netherlands, Belgium and Norway after failing to gain a single point from their six matches.

• Iceland finally managed to get their first World Cup qualification win in 1978 by beating Northern Ireland 1-0 in Reykjavik.

• After decades of slow progress, Iceland almost made it to the 2014 finals in Brazil. Their qualifying campaign featured a 4-4 draw away to Switzerland after they trailed 4-1, and they eventually finished second in the group behind the Swiss. That earned Iceland a play-off with Croatia, but the Balkan outfit proved too strong over the two legs, winning 2-0 on aggregate.

PREVIOUS TOURNAMENTS

1930 Did not enter	1966 Did not enter	1994 Did not qualify
1934 Did not enter	1970 Did not enter	1998 Did not qualify
1938 Did not enter	1974 Did not qualify	2002 Did not qualify
1950 Did not enter	1978 Did not qualify	2006 Did not qualify
1954 Entry not accepted	1982 Did not qualify	2010 Did not qualify
1958 Did not qualify	1986 Did not qualify	2014 Did not qualify
1962 Did not enter	1990 Did not qualify	

KEY PLAYER

GYLFI SIGURDSSON

In an industrious Iceland side full of energetic scrappers and tenacious tacklers, Everton's Gylfi Sigurdsson stands out as a player of real class. Elegant and composed on the ball, he is also renowned for his superb delivery at set-pieces and ability to strike spectacular goals from unlikely distances.

Now 28, the attacking midfielder has spent most of his career in Britain, making his name first as a teenager with Reading. In 2010 he moved on to German outfit Hoffenheim, before signing for Tottenham for £8.8 million two years later after an impressive loan spell at Swansea. He returned to south Wales in 2014 and his stock continued to rise as his goals and assists helped keep the Swans in the Premier League. In August 2017 he joined longtime admirers Everton for a club record £45 million, marking his full debut for the Toffees with an extraordinary 50-yard goal against Hajduk Split in the Europa League.

Sigurdsson was first capped by Iceland in 2010 and is now his country's third top scorer of all time with 18 goals.

CROATIA

Since finishing third at their first ever appearance at the finals in 1998, Croatia have become World Cup regulars and are usually one of the most entertaining countries to watch. That should certainly be the case again in Russia, given that the Croats possess two of the most talented midfielders of their generation in Real Madrid's Luka Modric and Barcelona's Ivan Rakitic.

However, the Croatia squad is an ageing one and there are concerns that this may be a tournament too far for some of their older players. A rather stuttering qualification campaign did nothing to allay those fears, a run of poor results costing manager Ante Cacic his job before the vital final group match away to Ukraine. Thanks to two goals from former Leicester City striker Andrej Kramaric, now with Hoffenheim, new boss Zlatko Dalic began with a win and Croatia clinched second place behind table-toppers Iceland. Then, in the play-offs, they were simply too good for Greece, winning 4-1 on aggregate.

> "I think we can navigate our way into the knockout stage, but it's going to be tough."
>
> Croatia coach Zlatko Dalic

With a starting line-up consisting mainly of players in their late twenties and early thirties, Croatia won't be lacking experience in Russia. In goal, Monaco's Danijel Subasic is steady and reliable, while Liverpool's Dejan Lovren is the key man in a well-drilled defensive unit. It's in midfield, however, that the Balkan outfit really sparkle, the central pairing of Modric and Rakitic providing a perfect blend of creativity, solidity, inspiration and perspiration. Meanwhile, nippy winger Ivan Perisic of Inter Milan, a recent transfer target for Manchester United, is another player capable of creating gilt-edged chances for Croatia's main striker, Mario Mandzukic. Mandzukic will be 32 come the finals so much will depend on the Juventus man retaining the sharp reactions inside the penalty area that have served him so well in the past.

CROATIA AT THE WORLD CUP

• Formerly part of Yugoslavia, Croatia first competed at the World Cup in France in 1998. They did brilliantly, too, beating Germany 3-0 in the quarter-finals before losing a tight semi-final 2-1 to the host nation. With six goals, Croatia striker Davor Suker was top scorer at the tournament.

• Croatia fared less well at the 2002 tournament, a surprise 1-0 defeat to Ecuador ending their hopes of reaching the knockout phase after they had recorded a good 2-1 win against Italy.

• In 2006 Croatia needed to beat Australia in their last group game to make it into the second round, but were held to a 2-2 draw. The match ended in remarkably bizarre circumstances when Croatia's Josip Simunic was only sent off by hapless English referee Graham Poll after being shown three yellow cards.

• On their last appearance at the finals in 2014, Croatia lost their first match 3-1 to hosts Brazil then thrashed Cameroon 4-0. That set up a 'win or bust' final game against Mexico which, sadly for the Croats, they lost 3-1.

PREVIOUS TOURNAMENTS

1930-90 Competed as part of Yugoslavia
1994 Did not enter

1998 Third place
2002 Round 1
2006 Round 1

2010 Did not qualify
2014 Round 1

KEY PLAYER

LUKA MODRIC

Nicknamed 'the Croatian Cruyff' in his home country for his ability to dictate the tempo of a game with his razor-sharp passing in all areas of the pitch, floppy-haired midfielder Luka Modric has been the seminal figure in the Croatia national team for well over a decade. It's no exaggeration to say that if he plays to his maximum in Russia then his side will have every chance of progressing to the knockout phase.

Croatian Footballer of the Year on six occasions, Modric became the first player from his country to be included in the Fifa World XI in 2015, repeating this feat in both 2016 and 2017. He is also the only Croatian player to have scored at two European Championships, in 2008 and 2016.

At club level Modric has won the Champions League three times with Real Madrid, most recently in 2017 following the Spanish giants' 4-1 thrashing of Juventus in the final in Cardiff, having joined the Spanish giants from Tottenham for around £33 million in 2012.

Prior to that the diminutive playmaker starred for Croatian side Dinamo Zagreb with whom he won three league titles before moving to north London in 2008 for £16.5 million, equalling Tottenham's transfer record at the time.

NIGERIA

Nigeria will be appearing at the World Cup for the sixth time in Russia, a record only bettered among African nations by Cameroon. The Super Eagles have fared reasonably well at the finals in the past, too, and will hope to reach the knockout stage as they did in 1994, 1998 and 2014. First they must negotiate a tough group which, incredibly, pits Nigeria against Argentina for the fifth time at a World Cup.

The west Africans have reason to be optimistic. Nigeria's form in qualifying was impressive, Gernot Rohr's side remaining undefeated in their final six group games as they topped the table by five points and eliminated 2017 African champions Cameroon. Then, in November 2017, the Super Eagles made the football world sit up when they came back from two goals down to defeat Argentina 4-2 in a friendly, Arsenal's Alex Iwobi scoring twice.

Nigeria's strength lies largely in midfield where captain John Obi Mikel, a Champions League winner with Chelsea in 2012, is supported by the likes of the energetic Iwobi, Leicester City's Wilfred Ndidi and the speedy Victor Moses. Up front, Rohr, an experienced manager who has taken charge of clubs in France and Switzerland as well as three other African national teams, can call on the muscular services of former Watford hitman Odion Ighalo as well as the Leicester duo Ahmed Musa and Kelechi Iheanacho. The latter pair, though, might be a bit rusty after playing second fiddle for most of the 2017/18 season to the number one striker at the King Power, England's Jamie Vardy.

Nigeria's defensive unit, meanwhile, is mostly made up of young players, with the exception of 30-year-old Elderson Echiejile. If the Super Eagles are to extend their stay in Russia the Sivasspor left-back's experience could well prove vital. In what promises to be an extremely tight group, Nigeria could just sneak into the top two.

> **"We will do our best and it will be a wonderful adventure."**
> Nigeria coach
> Gernot Rohr

NIGERIA AT THE WORLD CUP

• Nigeria first competed at the World Cup finals in the USA in 1994 and, to the delight of their fans, performed superbly. Victories against Bulgaria and Greece took the Super Eagles into the knockout phase where they gave eventual finalists Italy a scare in the last 16 before two goals from pony-tailed striker Roberto Baggio condemned them to a 2-1 defeat after extra-time.

• **Four years later Nigeria again made it out of the group stage after impressive victories over Spain and Bulgaria. However, a disappointing display against Denmark in the last 16 saw the Super Eagles crushed 4-1.**

• At the 2002 and 2010 finals Nigeria fared less well, on both occasions finishing bottom of their group after picking up just a solitary point from their three games.

• **However, in 2014 in Brazil the Super Eagles again reached the knockout phase, thanks mainly to a 1-0 win against Bosnia and Herzegovina courtesy of a Peter Odemwingie strike, before a 2-0 defeat to France in the last 16 ended their World Cup dreams.**

PREVIOUS TOURNAMENTS

1930 Did not enter	1966 Withdrew	1994 Round 2
1934 Did not enter	1970 Did not qualify	1998 Round 2
1938 Did not enter	1974 Did not qualify	2002 Round 1
1950 Did not enter	1978 Did not qualify	2006 Did not qualify
1954 Did not enter	1982 Did not qualify	2010 Round 1
1958 Did not enter	1986 Did not qualify	2014 Round 2
1962 Did not qualify	1990 Did not qualify	

KEY PLAYER

VICTOR MOSES

Nigeria fans will be hoping that Victor Moses shows the same form in Russia as he demonstrated throughout the 2016/17 season, when his dynamic, hard-running displays at right wing-back were one of the outstanding features of Chelsea's Premier League title-winning campaign.

Born in Lagos, Moses came to England as an 11-year-old after both his parents were killed in religious riots in Nigeria. After impressing as a schoolboy he was signed up by Crystal Palace, where his eye-catching performances attracted the attention of Wigan, who he joined in 2010. Two years later he moved to Stamford Bridge, but after a decent first season in west London he slipped down the pecking order and was sent out on loan to Liverpool, Stoke and West Ham, before his Chelsea career was revived by newly appointed Blues boss Antonio Conte in 2016.

Moses represented England at Under-16 to Under-21 level but decided to switch his international allegiance to Nigeria in 2011. He helped the Super Eagles win the Africa Cup of Nations in 2013 and represented his country at the 2014 World Cup in Brazil.

BRAZIL

After the trauma of that humiliating 7-1 defeat to Germany on home soil in the semi-finals of the last World Cup, five-times champions Brazil are back in business in spectacular fashion. Indeed, following an impressive qualification campaign, the South Americans have been installed as joint favourites to lift the trophy and their fanatical drum-beating supporters will surely head to Russia in confident mood.

Mind you, the hangover from 2014 took a little while to clear. After just two wins in their opening six qualifiers 1994 World Cup-winning captain Dunga was replaced as coach by Corinthians boss Tite. An excellent man-manager, he had an immediate impact on a squad suffering from low morale, and after a string of victories Brazil ended up topping the CONMEBOL group by 10 clear points. Mixing defensive organisation with creative flair, Tite's side were simply too strong for their opponents and, crucially, they did not depend solely on the brilliant Neymar for goals.

> **"These are top-class adversaries and that's why they are here."**
> Brazil coach
> Tite

Among those to chip in with useful contributions were Manchester City's Gabriel Jesus – who will battle with Liverpool's Roberto Firmino for the role of lone striker in a 4-1-4-1 formation – and Paulinho, a flop at Tottenham but now impressing at Barcelona. Gifted attacking midfielder Philippe Coutinho is another goal threat, as is Chelsea's slippery wideman Willian, although he may have to be content with a place on the bench. In Russia, though, most eyes will be on Neymar, Paris Saint-Germain's £200 million superstar, who will be determined to demonstrate that he is now the world's best player.

Neymar's cause will be helped if Brazil triumph for a record sixth time, and with a much tighter defence than the one which imploded so spectacularly last time out the South Americans will certainly be there or thereabouts.

THE GAFFER
TITE

Since he was appointed boss of Brazil in June 2016, Tite has transformed the South Americans' fortunes. After a scratchy start to their qualifying campaign under his predecessor Dunga, the 56-year-old oversaw 10 wins and two draws in the remaining matches as Brazil became the first country other than the hosts to book their place in Russia.

What's more, Tite replaced Dunga's counter-attacking style with a more attractive, possession-based style of football which has gone down well with fans and pundits alike and raised hopes that Brazil can claim the World Cup trophy for the first time since 2002.

In a long managerial career Tite – real name Adenor Leonardo Bacchi – experienced his best moments with Sao Paulo giants Corinthians. In 2012 he led them to the Copa Libertadores final, which they won with a 3-1 aggregate victory over Argentina's Boca Juniors. Later that year he raised more silverware when Corinthians beat Chelsea 1-0 in the final of the Club World Cup in Yokohama. A charismatic figure who thinks deeply about the game, Tite took a one-year sabbatical from his club in 2013 to study the latest developments in football tactics, before returning to Corinthians and leading them to the Brazilian league title in 2015.

KEY PLAYER

MIRANDA

Brazil may have a star-studded attack but if they are to lift the trophy in Russia their defence will need to be a lot stronger than it was at the last World Cup on their own home soil. That's why Miranda, a ball-playing centre-back who reads the game brilliantly, is such an important figure for his country.

Joao Miranda de Souza Filho, to give him his full name, made his international debut in 2009 but only really cemented his place in the Brazil side at the 2015 Copa America. The following year he captained the South Americans at the centenary edition of the same tournament.

At club level, Miranda won three league titles with Sao Paulo before joining Atletico Madrid with whom he won La Liga and reached the Champions League final in 2014. The following year he joined Inter Milan, where he continues to ply his trade.

Composed and blessed with excellent distribution, Miranda should prove vital to Brazil's campaign.

ONE TO WATCH
GABRIEL JESUS

Still only 20, livewire Manchester City striker Gabriel Jesus proved his worth to Brazil in the World Cup qualifying campaign by topping his country's scoring charts with an impressive seven goals.

Quick, hardworking and versatile, Jesus started out with Palmeiras, one of the biggest clubs in his home city of Sao Paulo. In 2015 he was voted best newcomer in the Brazilian league and the following year he was named player of the season as Palmeiras won their first national league title for 22 years. His superb form attracted the interest of numerous European outfits, and in January 2017 he joined Manchester City for £27 million. He has since proved a revelation in the Premier League, scoring regularly as City set a new top-flight record by winning 18 consecutive league matches during the 2017/18 campaign.

Jesus was part of the Brazil side which lost 2-1 to Serbia in the final of the 2015 Under-20 World Cup and the following year he featured in the Brazil team which won gold at the Rio Olympics after beating Germany on penalties in the final.

TACTICS BOARD

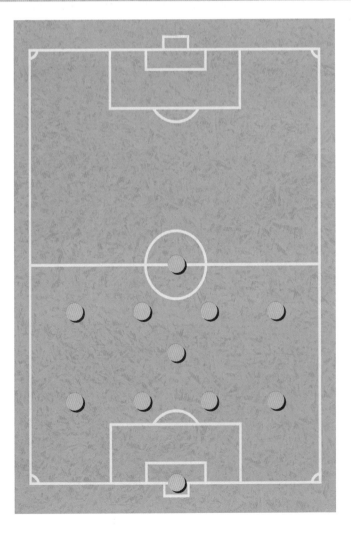

FOUNDATIONS FOR FORWARD FLAIR

Brazil coach Tite used both a 4-1-4-1 and a 4-3-3 formation in the World Cup qualifiers, with a slight preference for the former as it provides extra defensive solidity to complement the South Americans' natural flair.

In this system Real Madrid's Casemiro is an important figure, sitting just in front of the back four where he can break up opposition attacks and also get his team's own offensive movements started. Further ahead, the rejuvenated Paulinho, now with Barcelona, and the China-based Renato Augusto are two tireless workers while Philippe Coutinho and the iconic Neymar are free to flit around dangerously from their starting positions on the right and left respectively. Their intricate combinations with the lone striker, in all likelihood Manchester City's Gabriel Jesus, are central to Brazil's attacking play. So, too, are the forward surges of full-backs Marcelo and Dani Alves, both of whom can be considered virtually auxiliary wingers.

BRAZIL AT THE WORLD CUP

Brazil celebrate one of Ronaldo's two goals in the 2002 final against Germany

skipper Carlos Alberto and midfield maestro Gerson won the trophy for an unprecedented third time in Mexico in 1970. Flying winger Jairzinho scored in every round, including a 4-1 demolition of Italy in the final – a feat no player has matched since.

• **After an agonising 24-year wait, Brazil won the World Cup for a fourth time in the USA in 1994. Again, Italy were their opponents in the final, but this time the South Americans only tasted victory after the penalty shoot-out following a sterile 0-0 draw.**

• Brazil first competed at the World Cup in 1930, but failed to get out of their group after losing 2-1 to Yugoslavia. However, the South American giants did record their first win at the finals with a 4-0 hammering of Bolivia.

• The Brazilians finally got their hands on the trophy in 1958 when they beat hosts Sweden 5-2 in the final in Stockholm. Two of their goals were scored by an unknown 17-year-old striker called Pele, who became the youngest ever World Cup winner.

• A record fifth trophy followed in 2002 when Brazil beat Germany 2-0 in the final in Yokohama. Gap-toothed striker Ronaldo helped himself to both goals and, at the next tournament in Germany, took his total World Cup tally to a then record 15 goals, one ahead of Gerd Muller.

• **As hosts in 1950 Brazil only needed to draw with Uruguay in the last match of the final four-team pool to win the trophy for the first time. Filled to bursting point, the Maracana Stadium in Rio erupted when the home side took the lead just after half-time, but Uruguay responded with two goals to pip Brazil to the title.**

• **Four years later Brazil retained their trophy in Chile, beating Czechoslovakia 3-1 in the final in Santiago. The Brazilians' star player was winger Garrincha, who had overcome polio as a child to become a dazzling dribbler.**

• A brilliantly flamboyant Brazilian side containing the likes of Pele,

• **The only country to appear at all 20 previous finals, Brazil hosted the World Cup for a second time in 2014. Backed by their passionate fans the South Americans saw off Chile and Colombia in the first two knockout rounds before suffering a catastrophic 7-1 defeat in the semi-final at the hands of an utterly rampant Germany.**

PREVIOUS TOURNAMENTS

1930 Round 1	1966 Round 1	1994 Winners
1934 Round 1	1970 Winners	1998 Runners up
1938 Semi-finals	1974 Fourth place	2002 Winners
1950 Runners up	1978 Third place	2006 Quarter-finals
1954 Quarter-finals	1982 Round 2	2010 Quarter-finals
1958 Winners	1986 Quarter-finals	2014 Fourth place
1962 Winners	1990 Round 2	

SWITZERLAND

Switzerland have become World Cup regulars since the start of the new millennium and will be appearing at their fourth consecutive finals in Russia. Boasting a relatively young squad, the Swiss will hope to progress from a competitive-looking group but their ultimate aim must be to win a knockout match, something they have not managed since hosting the tournament way back in 1954.

Led by Vladimir Petkovic, a Bosnian who previously managed Lazio to success in the Coppa Italia in 2013, the Swiss won their first nine qualifiers but were pipped to top spot in their group by Portugal after a final-day 2-0 defeat in Lisbon. Condemned to the play-offs, Switzerland then made heavy weather of beating Northern Ireland, scraping through 1-0 on aggregate thanks to a highly controversial penalty converted by Milan left-back Ricardo Rodriguez.

> **"Brazil are not the only opponents in the group, the others are also difficult."**
> Switzerland coach
> Vladimir Petkovic

Still, those patchy displays will be forgotten if the Swiss perform to their best this summer. Primarily an obdurate, well-organised and disciplined unit, Switzerland also possess a touch of flair in the shape of Stoke's mini maestro Xherdan Shaqiri. If fit, fellow playmaker Valon Behrami, now with Udinese after spells at West Ham and Watford, is also easy on the eye while Arsenal's Granit Xhaka adds steel to the midfield mix. Opponents should also be wary of skipper Stephan Lichtsteiner of Juventus who, even at 34, still makes his trademark surging runs from right-back which have earned him the playful nickname 'The Swiss Express'.

With a strong central defensive partnership in Basel's Manuel Akanji and Deportivo la Coruna's Fabian Schar, Switzerland won't concede many goals. Whether they will score enough themselves remains a concern, especially as main striker Haris Seferovic of Benfica looks to be short of the required quality at international level.

SWITZERLAND AT THE WORLD CUP

• Switzerland have reached the quarter-finals of the World Cup on three occasions, the last time as hosts in 1954 when they were beaten 7-5 by Austria in the highest-scoring match ever to take place at a World Cup.

• Following a 24-year absence from the world stage Switzerland qualified for USA '94 under their English coach, Roy Hodgson. They performed reasonably well, too, reaching the second round before losing 3-0 to Spain.

• In 2006 Switzerland became the first ever team to be knocked out of the World Cup without conceding a single goal. After a 0-0 draw with France, the Swiss then beat both Togo and South Korea 2-0 to reach the knock-out stage. A fourth clean sheet followed against Ukraine in the last 16, but the Swiss were beaten in the tense shoot-out following another 0-0 draw.

• At their last appearance at the finals in Brazil in 2014, Switzerland again made it through to the last 16, thanks mainly to a Xherdan Shaqiri hat-trick against Honduras. However, a 1-0 defeat by Argentina ended their hopes of further progress.

PREVIOUS TOURNAMENTS

1930 Did not enter	1966 Round 1	1994 Round 2
1934 Quarter-finals	1970 Did not qualify	1998 Did not qualify
1938 Quarter-finals	1974 Did not qualify	2002 Did not qualify
1950 Round 1	1978 Did not qualify	2006 Round 2
1954 Quarter-finals	1982 Did not qualify	2010 Round 1
1958 Did not qualify	1986 Did not qualify	2014 Round 2
1962 Round 1	1990 Round 2	

KEY PLAYER

XHERDAN SHAQIRI

A beautifully balanced creative midfielder who is adept at dribbling past opponents and can score spectacular goals, Xherdan Shaqiri is the standout star in an otherwise rather functional Swiss team.

Born in Kosovo in 1991, Shaqiri moved with his ethnic Albanian parents to Switzerland the following year when war broke out in his homeland. He came through the youth ranks at Basel to make his first-team debut as a 17-year-old and won three league titles before joining Bayern Munich in 2012. In his first season in Bavaria he helped Bayern win the treble, although he didn't get off the bench in their Champions League final victory against Borussia Dortmund.

In January 2015 Shaqiri joined Inter Milan but only spent six months in Italy before moving to Stoke for a then club record £12 million. He has since become a firm favourite at the Britannia for his subtle passing and long-range shooting.

Swiss Player of the Year in 2012, Shaqiri made his international debut in 2010 and has gone on to win over 60 caps for his country, scoring 20 goals.

COSTA RICA

Costa Rica were the surprise packages of the last World Cup in Brazil, topping a tough group ahead of Uruguay, Italy and England before marching on to the quarter-finals where they were unlucky to lose to the Netherlands in a penalty shoot-out. Los Ticos, as they are known to their fans, are unlikely to do as well in Russia but their recent record means they should not be underestimated.

Many of the heroes of 2014 are still in a squad which is hugely experienced in international terms, but perhaps lacking a little in youthful promise. Possibly the team's most famous figure is goalkeeper Keylor Navas, a two-time Champions League winner with Real Madrid in 2016 and 2017. In front of him, the defence includes two British-based players in Sunderland left-back Bryan Oviedo, now recovered from a double fracture of the leg sustained with Everton, and Celtic right-back Cristian Gamboa. There is another familiar face in midfield in the form of former Fulham star Bryan Ruiz, the captain of the side. With his height, he represents a significant

> **"Brazil will be tough, given their history. But we're pleased with our group."**
> Costa Rica coach
> Oscar Ramirez

goal threat from set pieces, but Los Ticos' main attacking weapon is striker Joel Campbell, currently on loan at Real Betis from Arsenal.

Costa Rica are managed by Oscar Ramirez, who played for his country at their first World Cup appearance in Italy in 1990. He took over the reins in August 2015 after then boss Paulo Wanchope, once of Derby, West Ham and Manchester City, was forced to resign after fighting with a security guard during an Under-23 match against Panama.

Ramirez oversaw a solid qualification campaign, which saw Costa Rica secure their place in Russia when Vancouver Whitecaps centre-back Kendall Waston powered home an equalising header in Los Ticos' penultimate match against Honduras.

Costa Rica will fight hard, but a last 16 place looks beyond them this time.

COSTA RICA AT THE WORLD CUP

• At their first appearance at the finals in 1990, Costa Rica pulled off a major upset when they defeated Scotland 1-0 in their opening fixture. A 2-1 win over Sweden in their final group game booked Los Ticos' passage into the last 16, where they were routed 4-1 by Czechoslovakia.

• Costa Rica again did their country proud in 2002, beating China 2-0 and drawing 1-1 with eventual semi-finalists Turkey before a 5-2 loss against Brazil meant they were pipped to second place in their group by the Turks on goal difference.

• Four years later in Germany, Costa Rica fared less well, losing 4-2 to the home nation in the tournament's opening match, and then going down to both Ecuador (0-3) and Poland (1-2).

• On their last World Cup appearance in 2014, Costa Rica enjoyed shock group wins over Uruguay (3-1) and Italy (1-0) to secure their place in the last 16 where they beat Greece on penalties. However, their luck ran out against the Netherlands in their quarter-final, which they lost in another shoot-out. Still, Los Ticos returned to Costa Rica as national heroes.

PREVIOUS TOURNAMENTS

1930 Did not enter	1966 Did not qualify	1994 Did not qualify
1934 Did not enter	1970 Did not qualify	1998 Did not qualify
1938 Did not enter	1974 Did not qualify	2002 Round 1
1950 Did not enter	1978 Did not qualify	2006 Round 1
1954 Did not enter	1982 Did not qualify	2010 Did not qualify
1958 Did not qualify	1986 Did not qualify	2014 Quarter-finals
1962 Did not qualify	1990 Round 2	

KEY PLAYER

KEYLOR NAVAS

Real Madrid goalkeeper Keylor Navas was one of the unexpected stars of the last World Cup, earning three Man of the Match awards to help Costa Rica reach the quarter-finals of the competition for the first time in the country's history. Fans of Los Ticos will be hoping he can reproduce the same stunning form in Russia, although such is his worldwide reputation now few would be surprised if he doesn't perform even better.

An acrobatic shot-stopper with outstanding reflexes, Navas came to the fore with Spanish club Levante, winning the Goalkeeper of the Year award after a superb campaign in 2013/14. Real quickly snapped him up for a bargain £8 million, and after a year playing second fiddle to club legend Iker Casillas he claimed the gloves at the start of the 2015/16 season. Since then he has helped Real win the Champions League twice and the Spanish league in 2017.

Navas first played for Costa Rica in 2008 and is now one of the most experienced players in the side with nearly 80 caps to his name.

SERBIA

Serbia are making just their second appearance at the World Cup as an independent nation, having previously featured many times as part of Yugoslavia. The Balkan country came through a challenging qualifying campaign to book their place in the finals but will travel to Russia without the coach who guided them there, veteran boss Slavoljub Muslin having been unceremoniously axed in October 2017.

That decision seems particularly harsh given that Serbia finished above three strong sides – Austria, the Republic of Ireland and Euro 2016 semi-finalists Wales – to top their group. However, Muslin attracted criticism for some under-par performances and also for consistently leaving out highly-rated Lazio playmaker Sergej Milinkovic-Savic, so when he was replaced on a temporary basis by Mladen Krstajic it was not a complete surprise to fans of the White Eagles.

It remains unclear whether Krstajic, a former international defender in the days when Serbia was still united with Montenegro, will still be in charge this

> **"We have to improve in many departments if we are to make any impact at the World Cup."**
>
> Serbia captain
> Branislav Ivanovic

summer. However, whoever is at the helm will have a talented, if ageing, squad at his disposal. Experience runs through the team, especially in defence where captain Branislav Ivanovic, now with Zenit St Petersburg after a long and successful stint at Chelsea, lines up with Roma's Aleksandar Kolarov and Villarreal's Antonio Rukavina in a rugged back three ahead of a fourth thirty-something in goalkeeper Vladimir Stojkovic of FK Partizan.

In midfield, meanwhile, Manchester United's Nemanja Matic provides a muscular platform for Southampton's Dusan Tadic to demonstrate his mercurial skills. Serbia's attack is centred around Aleksandar Mitrovic, a burly and physically aggressive striker who was his country's top scorer in qualifying with six goals. If the Newcastle man can continue that good form in Russia a place in the last 16 is well within Serbia's grasp.

SERBIA AT THE WORLD CUP

• In their former guise of Yugoslavia, the team reached the semi-finals of the World Cup in both 1930 and 1962, losing to Uruguay and Czechoslovakia respectively.

• Following the wars in the Balkans in the early 1990s which saw the old Yugoslavia split into its constituent parts, a squad made up mostly of Serbian players competed at the 1998 World Cup as 'the Federation of Yugoslavia'. Narrow wins against Iran and the USA saw them reach the second round, where they went down 2-1 to the Netherlands.

• As 'Serbia and Montenegro' the Balkan side reached the 2006 finals in Germany in superb style, conceding just one goal in 10 qualifying games – easily the best defensive record in Europe. However, their much-vaunted backline collapsed in humiliating fashion at the tournament proper, where their three defeats included a chastening 6-0 thrashing by Argentina.

• As plain 'Serbia' they did slightly better on their last appearance at the finals in South Africa in 2010, a surprise 1-0 win over Germany being sandwiched between narrow defeats to Ghana and Australia.

PREVIOUS TOURNAMENTS

1930 Fourth place	1966 Did not qualify	1994 Banned
1934 Did not qualify	1970 Did not qualify	1998 Did not qualify
1938 Did not qualify	1974 Round 2	2002 Did not qualify
1950 Round 1	1978 Did not qualify	2006 Round 1
1954 Quarter-finals	1982 Round 1	2010 Round 1
1958 Quarter-finals	1986 Did not qualify	2014 Did not qualify
1962 Fourth place	1990 Quarter-finals	

KEY PLAYER

NEMANJA MATIC

One of the best defensive midfielders in the world, Nemanja Matic is a rock-like presence in the middle of the park, rarely losing a tackle and initiating numerous attacks with his astute and ultra-accurate passing.

Now 29, Matic started out as a playmaker with Slovakian outfit Kosice before joining Chelsea in 2009 for a bargain £1.5 million. Finding his chances restricted at Stamford Bridge, he moved on to Benfica in January 2011 in part-exchange for David Luiz, and blossomed in the Portuguese capital after being converted to a deeper midfield role. In 2013 he was voted Primeira Liga Player of the Year, prompting Chelsea to buy him back for £21 million the following January. Matic won two league titles with the Blues before making a surprise switch to Manchester United for £40 million in July 2017.

First capped by Serbia in 2008, Matic missed nearly a year of international football in 2013 after falling out with then boss Sinisa Mihajlovic. Since returning to to the fold, though, he has become the pivotal figure in the Serbian team.

GERMANY

Four-times winners and current World Cup holders, Germany will be among the favourites when the tournament kicks off in Russia this summer. Die Mannschaft, as they are known to fans, have a squad packed with top-notch players and are in tremendous form, enjoying a long unbeaten run stretching back to July 2016. The big question, then, is can Germany become the first country since Brazil in 1962 to retain their trophy?

Certainly, the signs provided by their qualification campaign were wholly positive. Joachim Low's men tore through their group, winning all 10 of their matches and scoring a joint European-record 43 goals in the process. Incredibly, no fewer than 21 different German players got on the scoresheet, demonstrating the team's ability to garner goals from all positions. For good measure, a squad largely made up of young players also won the 2017 Confederations Cup, beating Chile 1-0 in the final in Saint Petersburg.

> **"What we want to do in the group stage is set a foundation for the title defence."**
> Germany coach
> Joachim Low

Among the youngsters to impress in Russia were Schalke midfielder Leon Goretzka, Leipzig striker Timo Werner and marauding Bayern Munich right-back Joshua Kimmich, and this trio could force themselves into Low's starting line-up. The competition for places, though, is fierce, with even big names like Manchester City's Leroy Sane and Liverpool's Emre Can likely to be sat on the bench. The core of the team, meanwhile, will as usual feature a strong Bayern Munich presence, from goalkeeper Manuel Neuer through central defenders Mats Hummels and Jerome Boateng through to support striker Thomas Muller. Much, though, will depend on Mesut Ozil, the most creative player in Low's side but one who has been criticised for making little impact in big games for his club, Arsenal. Ozil, though, usually performs brilliantly for his country and if he is on song again the Germans will take some stopping in Russia. It will be a huge surprise if Low's men don't at least make the semi-finals.

THE GAFFER
JOACHIM LOW

In Russia this summer Germany boss Joachim Low will attempt to become the first manager since Italy's Vittorio Pozzo in 1938 to win consecutive World Cups. Given his track record and the superb squad at his disposal, Low must have every chance of emulating the legendary Italian.

Low was appointed as boss of his country in 2006, having previously worked as Jurgen Klinsmann's assistant. Since then his side has consistently challenged for honours, appearing in three major semi-finals and the final of the 2008 European Championships as well as claiming the biggest prize of all in Brazil four years ago.

Throughout his tenure, Low has made a point of blooding talented younger players while retaining a number of older heads with vast international experience. The current batch of youngsters are probably the most promising yet, prompting Low to send a squad with an average age of just 24 to the 2017 Confederations Cup. To nobody's great surprise the Germans won the tournament, playing the same swift and dynamic football Low has always advocated.

A workmanlike midfielder in his playing days, Low started out in full-time management with Stuttgart. His biggest success in club football away from the German giants came with Tirol Innsbruck, who he led to the Austrian title in 2002.

KEY PLAYER

MESUT OZIL

German national team Player of the Year on five occasions, Mesut Ozil is one of the most technically accomplished midfielders in the game. His superb passing ability, silky dribbling skills and composed finishing in front of goal will be vital to Germany's chances of retaining the World Cup in Russia.

Ozil first captured global attention in 2009 when was named Man of the Match and hailed as 'the German Messi' after the German Under-21 side smashed their English counterparts 4-0 in the European Championships final. In the same year he won the German Cup with Werder Bremen, scoring the winner in the final against Bayer Leverkusen.

After joining Real Madrid he won the Copa del Rey and La Liga with the Spanish titans, before joining Arsenal for a then club record £42.4 million in 2013. Ozil has since won the FA Cup three times with the Gunners, most recently in 2017.

ONE TO WATCH
TIMO WERNER

Tipped to be the next great German striker, 21-year-old Timo Werner has already made his mark at international level after winning the Golden Boot at the 2017 Confederations Cup and scoring seven times in his first 10 matches for his country.

Fleet-footed and quick to pounce on anything resembling a half-chance, Werner started out with his hometown club Stuttgart, becoming their youngest ever player when he made his debut in 2013 while still 17. Three years later Leipzig splashed out a club record £8 million to sign him, a fee which proved to be a bargain as Werner topped the list of German-born scorers in the 2016/17 Bundesliga campaign with an impressive 21 goals. However, he became something of a hate figure for supporters of other clubs when he dived to win a penalty in a match against Schalke.

That controversy led some German fans to boo Werner when he played in a World Cup qualifier against the Czech Republic in September 2017, but he answered his critics in the best way possible by opening the scoring after just four minutes.

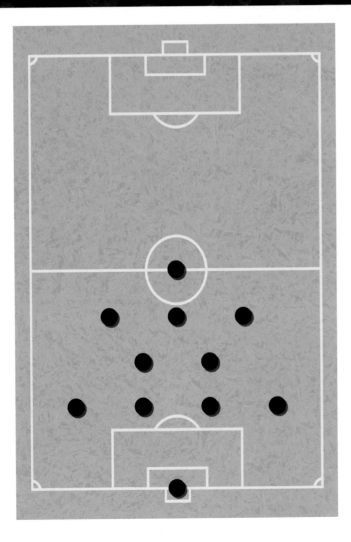

TACTICS BOARD

POWER PLAY

Positive in possession, adept at pressing and constantly looking to overload the opposition in wide areas, Germany are a clever, tactically astute side who threaten goals from all over the pitch.

Coach Joachim Low generally favours a 4-2-3-1 system, although he has sometimes experimented with an innovative strikerless formation in recent years. The emergence of young Timo Werner, though, means he has a natural leader of the line around whom to focus the attack, with Bayern Munich's Thomas Muller offering the Leipzig prodigy support from just behind and assistance in wider areas coming from the skilful Mesut Ozil and Paris Saint-Germain speedster Julian Draxler.

The technically excellent Toni Kroos keeps play ticking over from a deeper midfield position, while the two full-backs, Bayern Munich's Joshua Kimmich and FC Koln's Jonas Hector, are tasked with bombing forward as often as possible, leaving Bayern pair Mats Hummels and Jerome Boateng to mind the shop.

GERMANY AT THE WORLD CUP

• Germany first competed at the World Cup in 1934 and performed reasonably well, reaching the semi-finals before losing 3-1 to Czechoslovakia in Rome.

• **After being banned by Fifa from the 1950 tournament as a punishment for starting the Second World War, Germany returned to the world stage in 1954 (as West Germany) and won the trophy for the first time after coming from 2-0 down to beat Hungary 3-2 in the final in Berne. The result was a major surprise as the Hungarians had earlier trounced the Germans 8-3 in a group game.**

• West Germany reached the final for a second time in 1966, but went down 4-2 to hosts England at Wembley after extra-time. Nearly 50 years on, the Germans still complain that England's controversial third goal didn't actually cross the line.

• **Eight years later the Germans claimed the trophy for a second time when, as hosts, they beat the Netherlands 2-1 in Munich. Prolific striker Gerd 'der Bomber' Muller was the home side's hero, netting the winner after both teams had scored from the penalty spot.**

Germany's 2014 triumph clearly delighted Bastian Schweinsteiger and Lukas Podolski

• In 1982 West Germany reached the final for a fourth time, after beating France in the semi-finals in the first-ever World Cup shoot-out. However, a 3-1 defeat at the hands of Italy meant they headed home without the trophy.

• **Four years later West Germany were once again back in the final but lost again, this time going down 3-2 to an Argentina side inspired by their brilliant captain Diego Maradona.**

• The same two sides met again in the 1990 final in Rome, the Germans winning a bad-tempered match thanks to a late penalty by defender Andreas Brehme.

• **After shock quarter-final defeats by Bulgaria in 1994 and Croatia four years later, Germany reached their seventh final in 2002. The Germans had been indebted to their goalkeeper, Oliver Kahn, in previous matches but his blunder gifted Brazil their first goal in an eventual 2-0 victory in Yokohama.**

• Germany had to wait until 2014 before reaching the final again, but did so in style with a 7-1 thrashing of hosts Brazil in the semi-final – a match in which German striker Miroslav Klose set a new World Cup record by scoring his 16th goal at the tournament. In the final, Germany overcame Argentina 1-0 thanks to Mario Gotze's extra-time winner.

PREVIOUS TOURNAMENTS

1930 Did not enter	1966 Runners-up	1994 Quarter-finals
1934 Third place	1970 Third place	1998 Quarter-finals
1938 Round 1	1974 Winners	2002 Runners-up
1950 Banned	1978 Round 2	2006 Third place
1954 Winners	1982 Runners-up	2010 Third place
1958 Fourth place	1986 Runners-up	2014 Winners
1962 Quarter-finals	1990 Winners	

MEXICO

Mexico fans must be dreading the start of the knockout stage in Russia. Incredibly, for the last six World Cups their heroes have got out of their group only to fall in the last 16 – no more agonisingly then in Brazil four years ago when the central Americans led the Netherlands 1-0 with just a few minutes left on the clock only to concede two extremely late goals.

Mexico's qualification campaign suggests this may just be the year when they finally make it into the quarter-finals on foreign soil, their only two appearances in the last eight coming when they hosted the tournament in 1970 and 1986. 'El Tri', as they are known in reference to their tricolour flag, clinched their place in the finals with three games to spare and easily topped the CONCACAF group. Their results in the months since have been impressive, too, and include a 3-3 draw with Belgium and a win in Poland.

Appointed in October 2015, Colombian coach Juan Carlos Osario has made Mexico a much more consistent unit than in the past. However, he will need to control his notorious temper in Russia, having already been hit with a six-match ban by Fifa for insulting officials at the 2017 Confederations Cup.

His team generally play in a 4-3-3 formation, with the focus on a fast, attacking style that makes good use of widemen Jesus Corona of Porto and the highly-rated Hirving 'Chucky' Lozano. The PSV youngster is a classic inverted winger who loves to cut in from the left to shoot with his favoured right foot or look to slip in experienced goal poacher Javier 'Chicharito' Hernandez, now back in the Premier League with West Ham. Elsewhere, standout performers for Mexico include curly-haired goalkeeper Guillermo Ochoa, accomplished Roma centre-back Hector Moreno and captain Andres Guardado, an all-round central midfielder now with Betis.

> **"We are going to prepare very well so we can advance."**
> Mexico coach
> Juan Carlos Osorio

MEXICO AT THE WORLD CUP

• Mexico were the first country to host the World Cup twice. In 1970 the central Americans took advantage of playing on home soil to reach the quarter-finals for the first time in their history, at which stage they were trounced 4-1 by Italy. The Mexicans repeated that feat in 1986, when they took over hosting duties from the original choice, Colombia. This time West Germany knocked them out on penalties after a boring 0-0 draw.

• Fifa banned Mexico from the 1990 tournament after they fielded several over-age players at the 1988 CONCACAF Under-20 tournament in Guatemala.

• Since then Mexico have been remarkably consistent, reaching the last 16 at the previous six World Cups, including in 2014 when they were beaten 2-1 by the Netherlands after the Dutch grabbed two very late goals.

• Mexico goalkeeper Antonio Carbajal was the first player to appear at five consecutive World Cups, featuring for his country in the 1950, 1954, 1958, 1962 and 1966 tournaments. Less impressively, he conceded a joint-record 25 goals in the 11 games he played in.

• Defender Rafael Marquez's 16 World Cup appearances is a national record.

PREVIOUS TOURNAMENTS

1930 Round 1	1966 Round 1	1994 Round 2
1934 Did not qualify	1970 Quarter-finals	1998 Round 2
1938 Withdrew	1974 Did not qualify	2002 Round 2
1950 Round 1	1978 Round 1	2006 Round 2
1954 Round 1	1982 Did not qualify	2010 Round 2
1958 Round 1	1986 Quarter-finals	2014 Round 2
1962 Round 1	1990 Banned	

KEY PLAYER

JAVIER HERNANDEZ

A veteran of Mexico's 2010 and 2014 World Cup campaigns who is renowned for his ruthless finishing from close range, Javier Hernandez is his country's all-time leading scorer with an impressive 49 goals.

Nicknamed 'Chicharito' ('Little Pea') after his father, who was a Mexican international dubbed 'Chicharo' ('The Pea') because of his green eyes, Hernandez began his career with his local club, Guadalajara. He was signed by Manchester United for a bargain £8 million in 2010 and in four free-scoring seasons at Old Trafford helped the Red Devils win two Premier League titles and reach the Champions League final in 2011, which they lost 3-1 to Barcelona at Wembley. After a season-long loan spell with Real Madrid he moved on to Bayer Leverkusen in 2015, returning to England with West Ham two years later.

First capped by Mexico in 2009, Hernandez was named MVP after he topped the scoring charts at the 2011 Gold Cup, which Mexico won with a 4-2 victory over the USA in the final at the Rose Bowl.

SWEDEN

Sweden made it through to their first World Cup since 2006 in dramatic fashion, sensationally beating four-times winners Italy 1-0 on aggregate in the play-offs. That result was all the more remarkable as the workmanlike Scandinavians achieved it without their greatest ever player, Zlatan Ibrahimovic, who retired from international football in 2016. However, the charismatic Manchester United striker will surely be tempted to return to the world stage in Russia.

In some ways, it's a shame that the shadow of Ibrahimovic hangs over Sweden, because the spotlight should really be on the players who battled through a tough qualifying group, which included both France and the Netherlands, and then got the better of the Italians over two hard-fought legs. Credit must go too to 55-year-old manager Janne Andersson who has created a highly disciplined outfit which boasts a fantastic team spirit. Would the famously egotistical Ibrahimovic disrupt that unity and togetherness? It's a question Andersson will no doubt ponder at length before naming his final squad.

> **"Clearly Germany are the favourites, they are very good and a great footballing nation."**
> Sweden coach
> Janne Andersson

Sweden's main strength in qualification was in their defensive organisation, with just nine goals conceded in all 12 matches. Goalkeeper Robin Olsen of Copenhagen played his part in creating that impressive statistic, making some vital saves against the Italians especially. In front of him, captain Andreas Granqvist and Manchester United's Victor Lindelof are a solid centre-back pairing, with Celtic's Mikael Lustig a steady performer at right-back.

In midfield, the Swedes look to Leipzig wideman Emil Forsberg for a touch of flair, while Hull's Sebastian Larsson can be relied upon to deliver dangerous balls into the box at set-pieces. Up front, Andersson's compact 4-4-2 system allows for two strikers: one will almost certainly be the veteran Marcus Berg, but the identity of the other will be a hot talking point in Sweden over the coming weeks.

SWEDEN AT THE WORLD CUP

• Sweden made their World Cup debut in 1934, earning an impressive 3-2 victory over Argentina in their first ever match before losing 2-1 to Germany in the quarter-finals.

• Following fourth and third-place finishes in 1938 and 1950 respectively, Sweden hosted the 1958 tournament with high hopes. After topping their group, the Swedes beat the Soviet Union in the quarter-finals and West Germany in the semis to reach the final for the first time. The Rasunda Stadium in Stockholm was rocking when star player Nils Liedholm gave the home side an early lead against Brazil, but they ended up losing 5-2.

• Just once since then have Sweden threatened to lift the trophy. That was in 1994 when they faced Brazil in the semi-finals, only to lose 1-0 to the eventual winners.

• On their last appearance in the finals in 2006, Sweden clinched their place in the knockout phase with an exciting 2-2 draw with England. The Scandinavians, though, found it tough going against hosts Germany in the last 16 and went down to a 2-0 defeat in Munich.

PREVIOUS TOURNAMENTS

1930 Did not enter	1966 Did not qualify	1994 Third place
1934 Quarter-finals	1970 Round 1	1998 Did not qualify
1938 Fourth place	1974 Round 2	2002 Round 2
1950 Third place	1978 Round 1	2006 Round 2
1954 Did not qualify	1982 Did not qualify	2010 Did not qualify
1958 Runners-up	1986 Did not qualify	2014 Did not qualify
1962 Did not qualify	1990 Round 1	

KEY PLAYER

MARCUS BERG

Replacing the brilliant Zlatan Ibrahimovic was never going to be an easy task, but experienced striker Marcus Berg has given it a good shot. The burly forward was Sweden's top scorer in qualifying with eight goals, four of those coming in an 8-0 hammering of hapless minnows Luxembourg.

Strong in the air and packing a powerful shot in both feet, the 31-year-old now plays his football in the United Arab Emirates with Al Ain after an itinerant club career which saw him turn out for teams in Sweden, the Netherlands, Germany and Greece. He won the Swedish league with Gothenburg in 2007, finishing the campaign as joint top-scorer, and the Greek Cup with Panathinaikos in 2014, scoring a hat-trick in the final against PAOK. In his last season with the Athens club in 2016/17 he was top scorer in the Greek league with 22 goals.

At international level, Berg won his first cap in 2008 and the following year was voted Player of the Tournament after finishing as top scorer at the 2009 European Under-21 Championships with seven goals.

SOUTH KOREA

South Korea will make their ninth consecutive appearance at the World Cup in Russia this summer – a record of consistency which even the likes of England, Portugal and Uruguay can't match. Backed by their legions of red t-shirted fans, the Koreans stunned everybody by reaching the semi-finals when they co-hosted the tournament in 2002, but their chances of pulling off a similar surprise look extremely remote this time round.

The Reds squeaked through their qualifying group, finishing seven points behind table-toppers Iran and only securing their place in the finals by the skin of their teeth. A rather limp campaign led to a change of manager, with Shin Tae-yong, the former coach of South Korea's Under-20 and Under-23 teams, taking over from ex-Germany international Uli Stielike. 'The Asian Mourinho', as he has been dubbed, managed to steady the ship and a reshaped defence held firm to earn vital 0-0 draws with Iran and Uzbekistan in the Reds' last two games.

> **"The world will see how strong South Korea are at the World Cup."**
> South Korea coach
> Shin Tae-yong

The squad that Shin will take to Russia is thin on star names, and instead will largely rely on the traditional South Korean qualities of fighting spirit, good organisation and endless running. The one exception, of course, is Tottenham's Son Heung-min, who has emerged as a forward of genuine class in recent seasons. He will need support, though, and will look to the likes of Swansea's Ki Sung-yueng, the team's experienced captain, and Augsburg's Koo Ja-cheol to provide him with chances. Another play to watch out for is Lee Dong-gook. The former Middlesbrough striker will be 39 when the finals start but has a decent goalscoring record at international level.

However, the squad as a whole is pretty mediocre and it would be a surprise if the South Koreans make it out of their group.

SOUTH KOREA AT THE WORLD CUP

• South Korea's first World Cup experience in 1954 was a forgettable one as they were hammered 9-0 by Hungary – one of the heaviest defeats in the tournament's history. They did slightly better in their second game, however, suffering a mere 7-0 loss to Turkey.

• Co-hosting the 2002 finals with Japan, South Korea finally claimed their first World Cup win (at the 15th attempt) when they beat Poland 2-0. In the last 16 they sensationally beat Italy thanks to a late goal by Ahn Jung-hwan – who was then harshly sacked by his club, Perugia, for 'ruining' Italian football. After beating Spain on penalties, South Korea marched on to the semi-finals, where they lost 1-0 to Germany.

• In South Africa in 2010, South Korea reached the last 16 for a second time but fell victim to Luis Suarez, who grabbed both Uruguay's goals in his side's 2-1 win.

• South Korea performed less impressively in Brazil in 2014, picking up just a single point from a draw with Russia before losing to both Algeria and Belgium.

PREVIOUS TOURNAMENTS

1930 Did not enter	1966 Did not enter	1994 Round 1
1934 Did not enter	1970 Did not qualify	1998 Round 1
1938 Did not enter	1974 Did not qualify	2002 Fourth place
1950 Did not enter	1978 Did not qualify	2006 Round 1
1954 Round 1	1982 Did not qualify	2010 Round 2
1958 Entry not accepted	1986 Round 1	2014 Round 1
1962 Did not qualify	1990 Round 1	

KEY PLAYER

SON HEUNG-MIN

A workaholic frontman who loves to cut inside from the flanks before unleashing a piledriver, Son Heung-min will be South Korea's main goal threat in South Korea.

The most expensive Asian player ever when he moved from Bayer Leverkusen to Tottenham for £22 million in 2015, Son has taken his game to another level in north London and, although he has not always been a starter in the first team, has played a big role in Spurs' rise from also rans to Premier League title challengers. In 2016/17 he was joint-top scorer in that season's FA Cup competition with six goals, and the following campaign he became the leading Asian goalscorer in the history of the Premier League when he struck a superb winner against Crystal Palace at Tottenham's temporary Wembley home.

In 2015 Son was named Asian Footballer of the Year – the first South Korean to win this award – and in the same year was on the scoresheet in the Asian Cup final, but had to settle for a runners-up medal after Australia won 2-1 in extra-time.

BELGIUM

With a squad packed full of high-profile Premier League players, Belgium could go all the way this summer. Yet, the Red Devils have been tipped to do well at previous tournaments and then ultimately disappointed. Will the same story unfold in Russia or will Belgium finally deliver on their undoubted potential? Either way, it will be fascinating to follow their progress, especially as they have landed in the same group as England.

The signs in qualifying were certainly promising for Roberto Martinez's side. Not only did the Belgians top their group with ease, but they also banged in a joint European record 43 goals along the way. Muscular Manchester United striker Romelu Lukaku helped himself to 11 of those, a tally only bettered in the European section by Robert Lewandowski and Cristiano Ronaldo. Behind him, meanwhile, Chelsea's Eden Hazard and Manchester City's Kevin De Bruyne are two of the most creative attacking midfielders in the world, providing Belgium with an attacking trident that will simply terrify most defences.

> **"I think it is a varied group and epitomises what the World Cup is all about."**
> Belgium coach
> Roberto Martinez

Yet, the Red Devils still have some problems. After a rather shambolic 3-3 friendly draw with Mexico in November 2017 a furious De Bruyne was openly critical of Martinez's tactical approach. On paper, though, Belgium should be sound defensively as the Tottenham pair of Toby Alderweireld and Jan Vertonghen plus Manchester City's Vincent Kompany form a formidable back three. In front of them, Manchester United's Marouane Fellaini and Tottenham's Moussa Dembele are a solid and physically imposing pair of midfielders, while Chelsea's Thibaut Courtois is a reliable goalkeeper.

Belgium have the necessary quality in every position to make a huge impact, but do they have the right manager? Martinez is inexperienced at international level, and the Red Devils' chances may ultimately depend on how quickly he adapts to the particular demands and challenges of tournament football.

THE GAFFER
ROBERTO MARTINEZ

More than a few eyebrows were raised when Roberto Martinez was appointed as Belgium manager in August 2016, just a few months after he had been sacked by Everton following a second successive disappointing season at Goodison Park. However, the attack-minded Spaniard, ably assisted by France and Arsenal legend Thierry Henry, has proved to be a good fit for a squad packed full of exciting players and led Belgium through an impressive qualifying campaign.

The 44-year-old began his managerial career with Swansea City in 2007, a short while after playing for the club in a defensive midfield role. He was an instant success in south Wales, taking the Swans to the League One title in 2008 before deciding to join Premier League outfit Wigan Athletic, another of his former clubs, in 2009. Martinez enjoyed his greatest achievement yet with the Latics when they sensationally beat Manchester City in the 2013 FA Cup final at Wembley, thanks to a late headed goal by Ben Watson. However, just three days later Wigan were relegated to the Championship, ending their eight-year stint in the top flight. Martinez then joined Everton, leading the Toffees to their best ever Premier League points tally, 72, in 2013/14.

KEY PLAYER

KEVIN DE BRUYNE

Rated by many as the best midfielder in the world, Kevin De Bruyne can change the course of a match in an instant, whether it's with a surging run from deep, a defence-splitting pass or a thunderbolt from the edge of the box.

After starting out with Genk and then having short spells with Chelsea and Werder Bremen, the Tintin-lookalike upped his game at Wolfsburg, for whom he contributed a Bundesliga record 21 assists in the 2014/15 season and won the German Footballer of the Year award. His superb form prompted Manchester City to splash out a club record £55 million for his services in August 2015, since when he has become one of the most outstanding performers in the Premier League.

First capped in a friendly against Finland in 2010, De Bruyne was part of the Belgian team that reached the quarter-finals of both the 2014 World Cup and Euro 2016.

ONE TO WATCH
THOMAS MEUNIER

Belgium have so many high-profile players that right-back Thomas Meunier is in danger of going under the radar. However, it would be a mistake for opponents to underestimate the Paris Saint-Germain player, who demonstrated in qualifying that he carries a potent attacking threat.

Indeed, the 26-year-old even managed a hat-trick in Belgium's 9-0 destruction of minnows Gibraltar and ended the campaign with an impressive total of five goals and seven assists – stats which more defensive-minded wing-backs might struggle to achieve in an entire career.

Meunier, though, is an accomplished finisher who started out as a striker with third-tier outfit Virton. He was converted to right-back after moving to Bruges, with whom he won the Belgian Cup in 2015 and the league title a year later. In 2016 he signed for Paris Saint-Germain for around £6 million, but has since faced stiff competition for a starting berth from Serge Aurier, who has since moved to Tottenham, and Dani Alves.

First capped at international level in 2013, Meunier featured in the Belgium team that reached the quarter-finals of Euro 2016.

TACTICS BOARD

ED AND KEV SHOW

Under Robert Martinez, Belgium have settled on a 3-4-2-1 formation that gives their talented attacking players licence to create without worrying too much about defensive duties.

It's a system that is perfect for the twinkle-toed Eden Hazard, who loves to drift into spaces where his darting runs can create the greatest havoc. Alongside him, Kevin De Bruyne is adept at picking out powerful lone striker Romelu Lukaku with accurate passes or unleashing an unstoppable piledriver from distance. While Hazard and De Bruyne have the ability to dismantle any defence single-handed, Belgium also carry a threat from wide areas, especially on the right where pacy wing-back Thomas Meunier has a keen eye for goal.

In the centre of midfield, Belgium have strong options in Marouane Fellaini, Moussa Dembele and the feisty Radja Nainggolan of Roma, while the back three is likely to feature the seasoned Premier League trio of Toby Alderweireld, Vincent Kompany and Jan Vertonghen.

BELGIUM AT THE WORLD CUP

Marouane Fellaini in action for Belgium against Argentina in 2014

• Along with France, Romania and Yugoslavia, Belgium were one of just four European countries to appear at the first World Cup in Uruguay. The Red Devils, though, didn't have much to write home about after failing to score a single goal in defeats to the USA (3-0) and Paraguay (1-0).

• **Belgium played in the first of just two 4-4 draws in World Cup history in 1954, sharing eight goals with England in Basel, Switzerland. The Belgians were indebted to Portsmouth's Jimmy Dickinson who rounded off the scoring with a headed own goal.**

• Remarkably, the Belgians had to wait until 1970 before recording their first ever victory at the finals, a 3-0 defeat of minnows El Salvador. However, after losing 4-1 to the Soviet Union and 1-0 to hosts Mexico they were soon packing their bags for home.

• **In the opening match of the 1982 tournament in Spain, a single goal by Erwin Vandenbergh gave Belgium a surprise victory over reigning champions Argentina. For the first time the Red Devils progressed to the second round, where they lost both pool games to Poland and the Soviet Union.**

• Belgium's best ever showing at the World Cup came in 1986 in Mexico, when they came fourth. In the last 16 they saw off the Soviet Union in a 4-3 thriller, despite conceding a hat-trick to Igor Belanov. They then beat Spain on penalties before losing 2-0 to a Diego Maradona-inspired Argentina in the semi-finals. The Belgians' star man was skilful midfielder Enzo Scifo, who was named as the best young player at the tournament.

• **At the 1990 finals in Italy, Belgium were eliminated in the last 16 by one of the latest goals in World Cup history when England's David Platt struck a superb volley on the turn in the last minute of extra-time.**

• Four years later Belgian claimed a famous 1-0 win over neighbours the Netherlands in the group stage. In the second round, unfortunately, the Red Devils were beaten 3-2 by Germany in Chicago. There was some small consolation, however, for Belgium's Michel Preud'homme, who was named as the tournament's outstanding goalkeeper.

• **Belgium started the 2014 finals in Brazil in fine style, winning their first four games at a canter. However, in the quarter-finals they went down 1-0 to eventual runners-up Argentina.**

PREVIOUS TOURNAMENTS

1930 Round 1	1966 Did not qualify	1994 Round 2
1934 Round 1	1970 Round 1	1998 Round 1
1938 Round 1	1974 Did not qualify	2002 Round 2
1950 Withdrew	1978 Did not qualify	2006 Did not qualify
1954 Round 1	1982 Round 2	2010 Did not qualify
1958 Did not qualify	1986 Fourth place	2014 Quarter-finals
1962 Did not qualify	1990 Round 2	

PANAMA

Panama will be appearing at their first World Cup this summer, so it's little wonder that their successful qualification was greeted with wild scenes of celebration across the tiny central American republic. To add to the festive mood, the President announced that such a momentous occasion should be marked by a public holiday, so presumably there were a few hangovers when the Panamanians eventually stumbled back to work!

2017 CONCACAF GOLD CUP
PHILADELPHIA

Los Canaleros, as they are known in reference to the Panama Canal, made it to Russia thanks to an extraordinary victory in their final qualifier at home to Costa Rica. Trailing 1-0 at half-time, their chances of even claiming a play-off spot looked bleak before they grabbed a controversial equaliser, Guatemala-based striker Blas Perez's untidy attempt being awarded although the ball appeared to be cleared before it crossed the line. Then, with just two minutes left, skipper Roman Torres smacked home the winner. Panama's good fortune continued with the news that the USA had surprisingly lost to Trinidad and Tobago,

> **"We're very happy with the group because that's why we've come, to play the big teams."**
> Panama coach
> Hernan Dario Gomez

thus confirming Los Canaleros as the third automatic qualifiers in the CONCACAF section.

The unlikely combination of results meant that Panama coach Hernan Dario Gomez became only the second manager to lead three different countries to a World Cup, having previously performed the same trick with his native Colombia and Ecuador.

'El Bolillo' (The Baton), as he's known, can call on a highly experienced squad but one that lacks players plying their trade in the world's leading leagues. Among the key figures are goalkeeper Jaime Penedo of Dinamo Bucharest, a fixture between the sticks for Panama for more than a decade, and veteran striker Perez, his country's joint all-time top scorer with 43 goals.

They will be dogged and resilient, but it's hard to see Los Canaleros' lucky streak continuing in Russia this summer.

PANAMA AT THE WORLD CUP

• Panama have never appeared at the World Cup and didn't even enter the competition until the 1978 qualifying tournament. Los Canaleros got off to a great start, too, beating Costa Rica 3-2 at home before a series of defeats saw them finish bottom of their group.

• Four years later and there were no real signs of improvement as the Panamanians again propped up the rest of their group, claiming just a solitary point from their eight first-stage qualifiers.

• Panama continued to make little mark in world football until they reached the final CONCACAF qualifying group for the 2006 finals. However, Los Canaleros looked out of their depth, picking up just two points from their 10 games.

• It was a different story eight years later, though, as Panama came close to featuring in a play-off with New Zealand for a place at the 2014 finals. All seemed to be going to plan as Los Canaleros led already-qualified USA 2-1 in Panama City but unfortunately two injury-time goals by the visitors broke the hosts' hearts and handed the play-off slot to Mexico.

PREVIOUS TOURNAMENTS

1930 Did not enter	1966 Did not enter	1994 Did not qualify
1934 Did not enter	1970 Did not enter	1998 Did not qualify
1938 Did not enter	1974 Did not enter	2002 Did not qualify
1950 Did not enter	1978 Did not qualify	2006 Did not qualify
1954 Did not enter	1982 Did not qualify	2010 Did not qualify
1958 Did not enter	1986 Did not qualify	2014 Did not qualify
1962 Did not enter	1990 Did not qualify	

KEY PLAYER

ROMAN TORRES

Panama captain Roman Torres became a hero to his people when he smashed home a late winning goal against Costa Rica in October 2017 that clinched Los Canaleros' place at their very first World Cup. In Russia, though, the physically imposing and heavily tattooed central defender will be less concerned with scoring goals than keeping them out at the other end.

Now a 31-year-old veteran with over a century of caps, Torres started out with Chepo in Panama, before spending much of his career with clubs in Colombia. His combative performances and will to win caught the attention of a number of clubs in England, and in January 2012 he had a trial at Nottingham Forest. Despite impressing, no deal could be reached and Torres remained in South America.

In the summer of 2015 he moved on to Seattle Sounders, but almost immediately suffered a bad anterior cruciate ligament injury. He returned to action the following year, scoring the winning penalty in a shoot-out against Toronto that enabled Seattle to lift the MLS Cup for the first time in their history.

TUNISIA

Tunisia have appeared at four previous finals, although their past record has been pretty dismal: just one win in 12 matches in total. Their chances of progressing to the knockout stage this time also look slim as they have been drawn with two heavyweight countries in Belgium and England, but the north Africans will expect to pick up three points in their final match against minnows Panama.

'The Eagles of Carthage', as they are known to their fans, qualified in some style from their final group, remaining undefeated in six matches. It was no stroll, though, as they were pushed all the way by DR Congo and only secured their place in Russia with a nervy final-day 0-0 draw at home to Libya. Getting through the qualifiers was a personal triumph for head coach Nabil Maaloul, who had previously been in charge of Tunisia for just seven games in 2013, resigning after he failed to guide his country to the 2014 World Cup.

> "We have a chance. On paper Belgium are favourites in the group but second place will be contested by the Tunisia team and England."
>
> Tunisia coach
> Nabil Maaloul

The Eagles are a fairly young team on the whole, skippered by a 33-year-old veteran in the shape of goalkeeper Aymen Mathlouthi. He is rated as one of the best African keepers ever, but his fondness for dribbling around opponents inside his own penalty area has occasionally cost his side dear. In front of him, the defence is marshalled by another experienced figure, Aymen Abdennour. Currently on loan at Marseille from Valencia, he has in the past attracted the interest of Chelsea, Everton and Watford.

A more direct English link comes in the shape of attacking midfielder Wahbi Khazri, who is on loan at Rennes from Sunderland, after playing for the Black Cats in their disastrous 2016/17 Premier League relegation season. He will attempt to supply the bullets for star player Youssef Msakni, a striker with a delightful touch and a sharp eye for goal.

TUNISIA AT THE WORLD CUP

• Tunisia made their World Cup finals debut in 1978 and got off to a great start, beating Mexico 3-1. After a narrow defeat to Poland the north Africans needed to beat West Germany to progress from their group but could only manage a 0-0 draw.

• Tunisia returned to the world stage in 1998. In their first match against England, goals from Alan Shearer and Paul Scholes condemned them to a 2-0 defeat. Another loss to Colombia followed before they picked up a point in a 1-1 draw with Romania.

• Four years later Tunisia again managed just a solitary point from their three group games, thanks to a 1-1 draw with Belgium. However, 2-0 defeats to Russia and co-hosts Japan condemned them to last place in their group.

• Appearing at a third consecutive finals in Germany in 2006, Tunisia opened their account by drawing 2-2 with Saudi Arabia. They then took the lead against Spain before losing 3-1, and a 1-0 defeat to Ukraine meant they were home before the postcards yet again.

PREVIOUS TOURNAMENTS

1930-54 Competed as part of France	1978 Round 1	2006 Round 1
1958 Did not enter	1982 Did not qualify	2010 Did not qualify
1962 Did not qualify	1986 Did not qualify	2014 Did not qualify
1966 Withdrew	1990 Did not qualify	
1970 Did not qualify	1994 Did not qualify	
1974 Did not qualify	1998 Round 1	
	2002 Round 1	

KEY PLAYER

YOUSSEF MSAKNI

Dubbed 'the Arabic Messi' for his brilliant close control, superb dribbling skills and ability to finish with either foot, Youssef Msakni could be a surprise star of the 2018 finals.

The 27-year-old striker started out with Esperance Tunis in 2008. He went on to win four league titles with the club – topping the scoring charts with 17 goals in 2011/12 – and helped Esperance win the CAF Champions League in 2011. His excellent form saw him linked with a move to French giants Paris Saint-Germain and Monaco, but instead he joined Qatar Stars League club Lekhwiya (now known as Al-Duhail) for around £10 million in January 2013 – at the time a record fee for an African player. Later that year he scored for his new club in the Qatar Crown Prince Cup final in a 3-2 victory against Al Sadd.

Msakni made his debut for Tunisia in 2010 and now has over 50 caps for his country. His total of 14 international goals includes two hat-tricks, the second coming in a World Cup qualifier against Guinea in October 2017.

ENGLAND

Since their solitary World Cup triumph in 1966, England have managed just one semi-final appearance at the finals back in 1990. It's a pretty abysmal record for a country which claims to be 'the home of football' and also boasts the richest league in world football – albeit one stuffed full of overseas talent. Yet, after a kind draw, Gareth Southgate's squad will travel to Russia in a relatively confident mood.

England's recent performances, too, have been mildly encouraging, a young Three Lions side earning creditable 0-0 draws with reigning champions Germany and Brazil. Southgate can also point to a qualifying campaign which saw England comfortably top their group without losing a single match while conceding just three goals. However, less positively, some of the team's displays were laborious and turgid in the extreme, with fans even staging a protest walk-out during a flattering 4-0 win in Malta.

A lack of flair in central midfield is one issue Southgate needs to address, with neither Eric Dier nor Jordan Henderson convincing in a playmaker role. Arsenal's Jack Wilshere would be a more imaginative choice, provided he is fit and playing regularly. The Three Lions boss also faces a difficult decision in goal, with long-time first choice Joe Hart under increasing pressure from Everton's Jordan Pickford after losing form and confidence.

Up front, though, the picture is rosier with Harry Kane having emerged as a world-class striker in recent seasons. The support act around him is also impressive, with the likes of Kane's Spurs colleague Dele Alli and the nippy Raheem Sterling capable of producing moments of inspiration.

England should have no problems reaching the knockout stages, but after recent failures – notably the humiliating defeat to Iceland at Euro 2016 – it would be a brave fan who would back them going much further.

> "I think the Belgium game will capture the imagination back home as they have so many players in our league."
>
> England coach
> Gareth Southgate

THE GAFFER
GARETH SOUTHGATE

A calm, composed and thoughtful figure in the England dug-out, Gareth Southgate became manager of the Three Lions, initially on a four-match temporary basis following the sudden resignation of Sam Allardyce in September 2016. Now enjoying the security of a four-year contract, the 47-year-old has adapted well to his new role, guiding England through the qualifying stage of the 2018 World Cup while introducing younger players to the team and experimenting with different tactical systems.

Southgate began his managerial career with Middlesbrough in 2006, two years after he became the first Boro captain ever to lift a major trophy when the Teessiders won the League Cup. However, he was sacked in October 2009, a few months after failing to prevent Boro slipping out of the Premier League. In 2013 he became England Under-21 manager and two years later led his team to the finals of the European Under-21 Championships, where they finished bottom of their group.

A ball-playing centre-back in his playing days with Crystal Palace, Aston Villa and Middlesbrough, Southgate won 57 caps for England, but is best remembered for a penalty shoot-out miss against Germany which cost England a possible place in the final of Euro '96.

KEY PLAYER

DELE ALLI

With star striker Harry Kane likely to be a marked man this summer, the onus could well be on his Tottenham partner-in-crime Dele Alli to chip in with vital goals. The attacking midfielder is, in any case, a natural scorer himself, especially dangerous when making late runs into the opposition box to meet crosses hit towards the far post.

The PFA Young Player of the Year in both 2016 and 2017, Alli has enjoyed a stellar rise since making his debut for MK Dons as a 16-year-old in 2012, first gaining national attention when he was voted the Football League Player of the Year in 2015, the same year he joined Spurs for £5 million – a bargain if ever there was one.

Alli's superb displays for Tottenham soon earned him an England call up, and he marked his first start for the Three Lions with a blistering long-range strike against France in a friendly at Wembley in November 2015.

111

ONE TO WATCH
RAHEEM STERLING

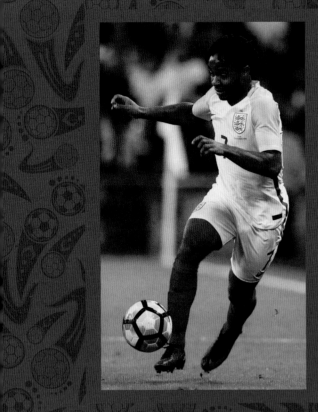

Currently enjoying his most prolific season yet in front of goal, speedy Manchester City winger Raheem Sterling will be hoping to replicate his dazzling club form with England this summer. Up to now the 24-year-old has struggled to make a major impact in international football, but such is his talent that could all change very quickly.

Jamaican-born Sterling started his career with QPR, before switching to Liverpool for a bargain £600,000 in 2010. Two years after breaking into the Reds' first team he won the 2014 Golden Boy award for the most promising player aged under 21 in European football.

In July 2015 Sterling joined Manchester City for £49 million, at the time the biggest fee ever paid for an English player. The following year he collected his first silverware with City when they beat Liverpool in the League Cup final.

Sterling made his full England debut in November 2012. In only his fourth game for the Three Lions he was sent off in a friendly against Ecuador to become the youngest ever England player to see red.

TACTICS BOARD

CREATIVE CONUNDRUM

England lined up in a 4-2-3-1 formation during most of the qualifying campaign, but in recent matches Gareth Southgate has recently adopted a 3-4-2-1 system which gives his side greater defensive solidity.

The most likely back three are Gary Cahill, Phil Jones and John Stones, with the latter's ability on the ball giving him the option of stepping into midfield at times. On the flanks England have pace in abundance, and both Danny Rose and Kyle Walker love getting forward to fire in dangerous crosses. Central midfield is a more problematic area for Southgate as neither Eric Dier or Jordan Henderson are particularly creative, and he might be tempted to recall Jack Wilshere if the nimble Arsenal ball-player is fully fit.

Up front, Dele Alli and one other – possibly Marcus Rashford, Adam Lallana or the in-form Raheem Sterling – will look to play in England's one true superstar, goalscoring phenomenon Harry Kane.

ENGLAND AT THE WORLD CUP

• Along with the other home countries, England declined to enter the World Cup in the 1930s following a dispute with Fifa about payments to amateur players. When England did finally make their debut in Brazil in 1950 they crashed out of the group stage after a shock 1-0 defeat to the USA – one of the biggest surprises in the tournament's history.

• **After reaching the quarter-finals in 1954 and 1962, England won the tournament on home soil in 1966. Geoff Hurst scored a hat-trick in the 4-2 defeat of West Germany in the final, including a highly controversial second in extra-time when his shot bounced down off the crossbar and on to or – as England fans always insist – just over the line. To the delight of the home fans, the referee gave the goal after consulting with one of his assistants.**

• England's defence of their trophy four years later got off to a nightmare start when, en route to Mexico, skipper Bobby Moore was arrested in Colombia on suspicion of stealing an expensive bracelet from a shop. He was eventually released to help England reach the quarter-finals, where they lost 3-2 to old rivals West Germany after extra-time.

England skipper Bobby Moore kisses the Jules Rimet trophy in 1966

• **England striker Gary Lineker's six goals at the 1986 tournament won him the Golden Boot, but Bobby Robson's team were eliminated in the quarter-finals by Argentina, thanks partly to the infamous 'Hand of God' goal by the South Americans' talismanic captain, Diego Maradona.**

• England had another dose of bad luck at the 1990 finals in Italy, going out on penalties to West Germany in the semi-finals. The Three Lions have since endured more shoot-out agony against Argentina in the last 16 in 1998, and against Portugal in the quarter-finals in 2006.

• England performed poorly in South Africa in 2010, only just making it out of the group stage and then losing 4-1 to Germany in the last 16. It might have been different, though, if the officials hadn't ruled out a clear Frank Lampard 'goal' when his shot bounced down off the crossbar and well over the line.

• Roy Hodgson's England fared even worse in Brazil in 2014, losing 2-1 to both Italy and Uruguay before drawing 0-0 with group table-toppers Costa Rica to round off the Three Lions' worst ever showing at the finals.

PREVIOUS TOURNAMENTS

1930 Did not enter	1966 Winners	1994 Did not qualify
1934 Did not enter	1970 Quarter-finals	1998 Round 2
1938 Did not enter	1974 Did not qualify	2002 Quarter-finals
1950 Round 1	1978 Did not qualify	2006 Quarter-finals
1954 Quarter-finals	1982 Round 2	2010 Round 2
1958 Round 1	1986 Quarter-finals	2014 Round 1
1962 Quarter-finals	1990 Fourth place	

POLAND

Despite missing out on the last two finals in Brazil and South Africa, Poland possess a decent World Cup pedigree, having come third in both 1974 and 1982. The Poles may not do quite as well this summer but they have the potential to be the tournament's dark horses, especially as they possess one of the most potent strikers in world football in Bayern Munich's Robert Lewandowski.

Although they didn't clinch their place in Russia until their final qualifying match – a 4-2 win against Montenegro in front of nearly 60,000 passionate fans in Warsaw – Poland topped their group in impressive style, finishing five points clear of second-placed Denmark. The Poles excellent form saw them promoted to the top pot of seeds for the World Cup draw – ahead of the likes of England, Spain and Uruguay – and they will certainly fancy their chances of progressing in a group that, on the face of it, includes no major threat.

Poland's strength lies in attack, with Hull's pacy winger Kamil Grosicki, Napoli's Piotr Zielinski and Wolfsburg's Jakub Blaszczykowski supporting the prolific Lewandowski in coach Adam Nawalka's attractive 4-2-3-1 formation. There are concerns, though, that the goals may dry up if the Poles' all-time top scorer is either injured or successfully shackled by opposition defences. The stats from the qualifiers tell their own story: while Lewandowski hit an astonishing 16 goals, of his teammates only Grosicki – with three – managed more than one.

Poland, though, are far from a one-man team and in nimble Juventus goalkeeper Wojciech Szczesny, combative Monaco centre-back Kamil Glik and fleet-footed Borussia Dortmund right-back Lukasz Piszczek they have a number of other top-notch players. As long as Lewandowski can keep banging in the goals, don't be surprised if they match their performance at Euro 2016 and reach the last eight.

> **"The players have proved themselves in difficult moments, and qualified in very good style."**
> Poland coach
> Adam Nawalka

POLAND AT THE WORLD CUP

• Poland made their World Cup debut in France in 1938. In their only match, striker Ernst Willimowski scored four goals but it wasn't enough as the unlucky Poles lost 6-5 after extra-time to Brazil.

• In 1974 Poland had a chance of reaching the final, but lost their decisive match in the second group stage to hosts West Germany on a rain-soaked pitch. However, the Poles claimed third place thanks to a goal by the tournament's top scorer, Grzegorz Lato, against Brazil.

• Poland reached the second group stage again in Argentina in 1978, but their hopes of making the final were dashed by a 3-1 defeat against Brazil. Four years later the Poles came through two group stages to reach the semi-final, but were undone by two goals from in-form Italy striker Paolo Rossi. Again, though, they took third place with a 3-2 win against France.

• Poland disappointed on their last World Cup appearance in 2006, losing to Ecuador and hosts Germany before they managed to narrowly beat Costa Rica 2-1 in their final game.

PREVIOUS TOURNAMENTS

1930 Did not enter	1966 Did not qualify	1994 Did not qualify
1934 Did not enter	1970 Did not qualify	1998 Did not qualify
1938 Round 1	1974 Third place	2002 Round 1
1950 Did not enter	1978 Round 2	2006 Round 1
1954 Did not enter	1982 Third place	2010 Did not qualify
1958 Did not qualify	1986 Round 2	2014 Did not qualify
1962 Did not qualify	1990 Did not qualify	

KEY PLAYER

ROBERT LEWANDOWSKI

A genuinely world-class striker, Robert Lewandowski is Poland's all-time leading scorer with over 50 goals for his country since making his debut in 2008. No fewer than 16 of those goals came in the Poles' World Cup qualification campaign for Russia, setting a new record for a European player.

Fast, strong and deadly inside the penalty area, Lewandowski made his name with Lech Poznan, with whom he topped the scoring charts when they won the Polish title in 2010. He moved on to Borussia Dortmund that summer, helping his new club win two league titles and the German Cup in 2012, when he scored a hat-trick in Borussia's 5-2 demolition of Bayern Munich in the final. The following season Lewandowski became the first player to score four goals in a Champions League semi-final, achieving this record in Dortmund's 4-1 thrashing of Real Madrid.

He signed for Bayern Munich in 2014 and has since won another three Bundesliga titles, enjoying his best season with the German giants in 2016/17 when he hit a career-best 54 goals for club and country.

115

SENEGAL

At their only previous finals in 2002, Senegal famously caused a major upset by beating reigning champions France on their way to the quarter-finals. Current coach Aliou Cisse, a Premier League player in his time with Birmingham City and Portsmouth, was the skipper of that legendary team and will not be lacking in inspirational World Cup stories to tell his players in Russia.

The Lions of Teranga, as they are known, demonstrated in their qualifying campaign that they are a capable all-round unit with some star quality up front, where Liverpool's Sadio Mane and West Ham's Diafra Sakho form a fearsome attacking partnership. Thanks in part to this duo, Senegal eventually won their group at a canter but only after enjoying a huge slice of luck along the way. In a decision which surprised many, Fifa annulled the Lions' 2-1 defeat away to South Africa after ruling that Ghanaian referee Joseph Lamptey had 'unlawfully influenced' the result by awarding the home side a controversial penalty for handball. The

> **"At first glance, people may say it's the easiest group, but in football nothing is easy."**
> Senegal coach
> Aliou Cisse

west Africans took advantage of the lifeline, winning the replayed match 2-0 a year later to book their passage to the finals.

Despite that stroke of good fortune, there is no doubt that Senegal deserved their place in Russia. Marshalled by giant Napoli centre-back Kalidou Koulibaly, the Lions have a strong defence, only conceding three goals in their six final qualifying group matches. In the centre of the park they are highly combative, thanks to the presence of West Ham midfielder Cheikhou Kouyate and Everton's Idrissa Gueye, the most prolific tackler in the Premier League in 2016/17. If that pair can supply the ammunition for Mane and Sakho then there is every chance that Senegal could match the heroes of 2002 by progressing out of their group — a group that appears to be intriguingly well-balanced.

SENEGAL AT THE WORLD CUP

• Senegal have only appeared at one previous World Cup, but they certainly made a huge mark at the 2002 tournament in Japan and South Korea. In their opening match in the Seoul World Cup Stadium against reigning champions France the Lions sensationally won 1-0 thanks to a goal by midfielder Papa Bouba Diop to record one of the biggest upsets ever in the history of the tournament.

• **In their next match Senegal drew 1-1 with Denmark, despite being reduced to 10 men when goalscorer Salif Diao of Liverpool was sent off 10 minutes from the end. The west Africans then raced into a 3-0 half-time lead against Uruguay, Diop scoring twice, before being pegged back to 3-3. The point, though, was enough to see the Lions through to the knockout stages.**

• In the last 16, Senegal came from behind to beat Sweden 2-1 in extra-time, the Lions' all-time top scorer Henri Camara grabbing both goals for the underdogs.

• Senegal's truly memorable World Cup adventure finally came to an end in the quarter-finals when they lost 1-0 to Turkey after extra-time in Osaka.

PREVIOUS TOURNAMENTS

1930 Did not enter	1966 Withdrew	1994 Did not qualify
1934 Did not enter	1970 Did not qualify	1998 Did not qualify
1938 Did not enter	1974 Did not qualify	2002 Quarter-finals
1950 Did not enter	1978 Did not qualify	2006 Did not qualify
1954 Did not enter	1982 Did not qualify	2010 Did not qualify
1958 Did not enter	1986 Did not qualify	2014 Did not qualify
1962 Did not enter	1990 Did not qualify	

KEY PLAYER

SADIO MANE

If Senegal are to progress in Russia they will need goals from their star man, Sadio Mane. A frighteningly quick player who usually finishes with aplomb, the Liverpool striker has been his country's main attacking threat since featuring at the 2012 Olympics in London. Five years later he helped the Lions reach the quarter-finals of the Africa Cup of Nations but missed a penalty in the shoot-out defeat against eventual winners Cameroon.

Mane started out with French club Metz before making his mark with Red Bull Salzburg, with whom he won the Austrian double in 2014. In the same year he joined Southampton for £11.8 million, hitting the headlines in May 2015 when he scored the fastest Premier League hat-trick ever in just two minutes and 56 seconds in a 6-1 defeat of Aston Villa.

In June 2016 he moved on to Liverpool for £34 million – the highest fee ever paid for an African footballer at the time – and enjoyed an excellent first season at Anfield, scoring 13 league goals and being voted into the PFA Team of the Year.

COLOMBIA

Colombia exceeded all expectations at the last World Cup, reaching the quarter-finals for the first time in their history before narrowly losing to hosts Brazil. The South Americans' patchy qualifying campaign suggests they will struggle to perform as well this time but, on the positive side, they have been drawn in a very even-looking group which no one country is likely to dominate.

Colombia's unimpressive form en route to Russia was mainly down to a lack of goals: just 21 in 18 matches. Fortunately 2014 Golden Boot winner James Rodriguez had his shooting boots on, contributing a vital six goals as Colombia sneaked into the last automatic qualifying place.

> **"We were worried about getting one of the big names. I wanted a balanced group and we've got that."**
> Colombia coach
> Jose Pekerman

Another factor behind the team's inconsistent showing was coach Jose Pekerman's inability to decide on his best starting XI. The defensively minded Argentinian called on the services of nearly 50 different players over the two-year qualifying period, baffling fans with some of his more unlikely call-ups.

Despite Pekerman's rather scattergun selection policy, it is not hard to predict who Colombia's most influential figures will be this summer. In goal, David Ospina is an excellent shot-stopper, although he may be a tad rusty after a season spent on the bench at Arsenal. The pacy and athletic Davinson Sanchez, also based in north London with Tottenham, has emerged as a young central defender of great promise since making his international debut two years ago. In midfield, Rodriguez is a talented creator who also carries a goal threat, while tricky winger Juan Cuadrado has got his career back on track with Juventus. The same can be said for Radamel Falcao, who is rejuvenated at Monaco after flopping with Manchester United and Chelsea having rediscovered his priceless ability to sniff out and convert the slimmest of chances.

COLOMBIA AT THE WORLD CUP

• Colombia first appeared at the World Cup in Chile in 1962. The South Americans came from 4-1 down to draw 4-4 with Russia, but defeats against Uruguay (1-2) and Yugoslavia (0-5) ensured that they finished bottom of their group.

• At Italia '90 Colombia made it into the second round after finishing as one of the best third-placed nations. However, a disastrous mistake by eccentric goalkeeper Rene Higuita gifted veteran Cameroon striker Roger Milla the decisive goal in the teams' last 16 meeting.

• Colombia's unexpectedly poor showing at USA '94 was overshadowed by the murder of defender Andres Escobar, who was shot dead by irate fans back in his homeland after scoring an own goal in a 2-1 defeat against the hosts.

• Thanks largely to the efforts of midfielder James Rodriguez, who won the tournament's Golden Boot, Colombia performed superbly at the finals in Brazil in 2014. After topping their group with three straight wins, Jose Pekerman's men comfortably beat Uruguay 2-0 in the last 16 – with Rodriguez grabbing both the goals – before narrowly going down to the hosts in the quarter-finals.

PREVIOUS TOURNAMENTS

1930 Did not enter	1966 Did not qualify	1994 Round 1
1934 Did not enter	1970 Did not qualify	1998 Round 1
1938 Withdrew	1974 Did not qualify	2002 Did not qualify
1950 Did not enter	1978 Did not qualify	2006 Did not qualify
1954 Banned	1982 Did not qualify	2010 Did not qualify
1958 Did not qualify	1986 Did not qualify	2014 Quarter-finals
1962 Round 1	1990 Round 2	

KEY PLAYER

JAMES RODRIGUEZ

Winner of the Golden Boot at the last World Cup in Brazil, James Rodriguez was in sharpshooting form again during the qualifiers for Russia and was Colombia's top scorer with six goals.

The attacking midfielder's excellent displays in international football, though, have been in stark contrast with his performances at club level since he moved to Real Madrid in 2014. Indeed, in the summer of 2017 the Spanish giants decided to dispense with his services for two whole years, sending him out on loan to Bayern Munich, where he has also struggled to shine.

Still, there is no doubt that Rodriguez is a major talent, possessing the ability both to score and set up goals from an attacking midfield role. His CV is a starry one, including a Portuguese Player of the Season award with Porto and a place in the Ligue 1 XI after a single season with Monaco in 2013/14.

His World Cup exploits also saw him voted into the 2014 World Cup All Star XI, while his wonderful volley against Uruguay won the Goal of the Tournament award.

JAPAN

Since qualifying for their first finals in 1998, Japan have become World Cup regulars, and in Russia will be appearing at their sixth consecutive tournament. The Blue Samurai, though, have generally struggled to make a big impact on the world stage, and will certainly be hoping to perform much better than their last outing in Brazil when they finished bottom of their group.

As one of the superpowers of Asian football, Japan usually breeze through the qualifiers. This time, though, they had a dreadful start to their final group campaign, surprisingly losing at home to the United Arab Emirates, before rallying to eventually top the Group B table just one point ahead of Saudi Arabia and Australia.

The squad put together by veteran coach Vahid Halilhodzic, a Bosnian who took Algeria into the knockout stage at the last World Cup, retains a number of familiar names from previous tournaments along with some promising younger players. The experienced hands include Metz goalkeeper Eiji Kawashima, Southampton centre-back Maya Yoshida and defensive midfielder and captain Makoto Hasebe. Meanwhile, much will be expected of two exciting novices, creative midfielder Yosuke Ideguchi, a transfer target for Leeds United, and Takuma Asano, a pacy wideman currently on loan at Stuttgart from Arsenal who Gunners boss Arsene Wenger has described as "one for the future".

Scoring goals has often been a problem for Japan, so it is something of a surprise that the Blue Samurai's most prolific striker, Leicester City's Shinji Okazaki, will probably start on the bench, with Cologne's Yuya Osako likely to start up front instead in a 4-3-3 formation. However, Okazaki will be a more than useful impact sub and his ability to harass and rattle defenders will likely serve Japan well in the closing stages of matches.

> **"We might have ended up with a much more difficult group. It looks like the most even group."**
> Japan coach
> Vahid Halilhodzic

JAPAN AT THE WORLD CUP

• Japan's World Cup debut in France in 1998 was one to forget as they slumped to consecutive defeats against Argentina, Croatia and Jamaica and only managed a single goal.

• The Blue Samurai did much better as co-hosts in 2002, reaching the last 16 after group-stage wins against Russia and Tunisia. However, a 1-0 defeat to eventual semi-finalists Turkey in the first knockout round shattered the mood of euphoria in the country.

• After a poor showing at the 2006 World Cup in Germany, Japan came good again in South Africa four years later. Wins against Cameroon and Denmark put the Blue Samurai in the last 16, where they played out a mind-numbingly tedious 0-0 draw with Paraguay before losing to the South Americans on penalties.

• Japan started brightly at the 2014 finals, taking the lead against Ivory Coast before going down to a 2-1 defeat. After a dull 0-0 draw with Greece, Japan had to beat Colombia to progress but, despite an equaliser from Shinji Okazaki, they were eventually beaten 4-1.

PREVIOUS TOURNAMENTS

1930 Did not enter	1966 Did not enter	1994 Did not qualify
1934 Did not enter	1970 Did not qualify	1998 Round 1
1938 Withdrew	1974 Did not qualify	2002 Round 2
1950 Banned	1978 Did not qualify	2006 Round 1
1954 Did not qualify	1982 Did not qualify	2010 Round 2
1958 Did not enter	1986 Did not qualify	2014 Round 1
1962 Did not qualify	1990 Did not qualify	

KEY PLAYER

MAYA YOSHIDA

A central defender who reads the game well and is comfortable on the ball, Southampton's Maya Yoshida is the most experienced figure in Japan's back four with nearly 80 caps to his name.

Now 29, Yoshida started out as a defensive midfielder with Nagoya Grampus but assumed a deeper role after stepping up to the first team. In March 2009 he scored the club's first ever goal in the AFC Champions League against South Korean outfit Ulsan Hyundai, before moving on to Dutch side VVV-Venlo. The highlight of his time in the Netherlands came in September 2011 when he powered home a magnificent bicycle kick against PSV Eindhoven, a strike which was voted the Dutch league's Goal of the Season. In August 2012 he signed for Southampton for a bargain £3 million.

Yoshida made his debut for Japan in 2010, and the following year helped his country win the Asian Cup for a record fourth time. He skippered the Blue Samurai at the 2012 Olympics and featured in all three of their games at the last World Cup.

CRISTIANO RONALDO

The Portuguese phenomenon has rewritten almost as many football records as he's scored goals and, with his fourth World Cup on the horizon, he's far from finished yet.

A forward who dominates every game he plays in, Ronaldo is already Real Madrid and Portugal's all-time leading marksmen, and with 21 major trophies and an array of individual awards on his CV already he's a player who has won virtually everything the game has to offer.

Ronaldo exploded on to the international scene at Euro 2004 when Portugal reached the final on home soil, and since his pyrotechnic introduction more than a decade ago he has proved himself one of the most deadly and destructive players football has ever seen.

Frighteningly fast and intimidatingly strong, Ronaldo's famous shooting ability and dead ball technique are perhaps his two greatest attributes, and with such an array of attacking weapons it is no surprise the star has already netted more than 500 times for Sporting Lisbon, Manchester United and Madrid and is now targeting an unprecedented century of goals for Portugal.

The winner of five coveted Ballon d'Or trophies awarded to the world's best player, as well as four Champions Leagues and three FIFA Club World Cup titles, the Portuguese star is a player who doesn't know the meaning of failure.

His international career began as a teenager in 2003 and he's now the country's most capped player, making his 147th appearance in October 2017 against Switzerland, having scored his 79th goal for Portugal three days earlier against Andorra. No player has made more appearances in the European Championship finals than Ronaldo's 21, and only the great Michel Platini of France can match his tally of nine goals.

Ronaldo's emergence on the world stage has sparked a golden era for his national team, and the crowning glory came in France in 2016 when his three goals inspired Portugal to victory in the European Championship, the first major trophy in the country's history.

The prolific Real Madrid forward is Portugal's all-time top goalscorer

STATS

DOB: **05/02/85**
Country: **Portugal**
International debut: **Kazakhstan, 20/08/03**
Caps: **147** Goals: **79**
World Cup finals appearances: **13 (2006, 2010, 2014)**
World Cup finals goals: **3**

HARRY KANE

The Tottenham Hotspur and England star has emerged as one of the game's most prolific and feared forwards since making his Premier League debut as a teenager back in 2012.

Strikers have always been football's most valuable commodity – clubs will invest millions to secure the services of a player who can find the back of the net on a regular basis – but Kane cost Spurs absolutely nothing, and after three record-breaking seasons for the Londoners the 24-year-old is worth his weight in gold.

Kane's meteoric rise began when he broke into the Spurs first team in the 2013/14 season, and ever since he's been banging in the goals for both club and country. His haul of 25 goals in 2015/16 made him the first Englishman to win the Premier League's coveted Golden Boot award for 16 years, an award he retained the following season.

The strength of his game is, to coin a phrase, his lack of weaknesses. Powerful on and off the ball, dangerous in the air and blessed with the vision normally associated with a midfield playmaker, Kane scores every type of goal and he's equally at home in the six-yard box as he is outside the area.

His senior England career began in March 2015 when he came off the bench in a Euro 2016 qualifier against Lithuania. The Spurs man needed just 79 seconds to open his international account with a header in a 4-0 victory for the Three Lions at Wembley, and from that moment he became one of the first names on the England team sheet.

Kane was his country's top scorer with five goals in qualifying for the 2018 World Cup, netting the winners in the all-important victories over Slovenia and Lithuania as well as a last-gasp equaliser against Scotland at Hampden Park, a game in which he wore the captain's armband for the first time.

Much is expected of Kane in Russia in 2018, but the Spurs player has already proved he has both the talent and temperament to live up to expectations.

When Tottenham Hotspur striker Harry Kane shoots... it's usually a goal!

STATS

DOB: **28/07/93**
Country: **England**
International debut: **Lithuania, 27/03/15**
Caps: **23** Goals: **12**
World Cup finals appearances: **0**
World Cup finals goals: **0**

LIONEL MESSI

The king of the Nou Camp, the Barcelona magician is the most prolific player in front of goal Spanish football has ever seen after 14 record-breaking seasons with the Catalan giants.

Messi was still two months short of his 18th birthday when he first found the back of the net for Barca. His maiden goal came in May 2005 in a league game against Albacete, and although the Nou Camp faithful knew they had an exciting new talent in their ranks few could have suspected just what an incredible impact the diminutive Argentinean would have on La Liga.

His strike was, of course, just the start of a flood of goals and he is now the league's all-time top scorer with more than 360 goals and counting. Messi is quite simply terrifying going forward and with him in their ranks Barcelona have enjoyed the most glittering period in the club's illustrious history. Eight league titles, five Copa del Reys, four Champions Leagues and three FIFA Club World Cups have all been lifted since the South American began his phenomenal career, and no one who witnessed his 73 goals in 60 appearances in all competitions in the 2011/12 season will ever forget his remarkable exploits.

A five-time Ballon d'Or winner, Messi's razor sharpness on the ball is matched only by his speed of thought, and his ability to ghost past bemused, stationary defenders is a joy to behold. His power-packed left foot is merely the icing on the cake.

Unsurprisingly Messi holds the record for the most international goals for Argentina. His hat-trick in the World Cup qualifier against Ecuador in October 2017 took his tally to 61 in 123 appearances, part of a superb solo display which secured Argentina's place in Russia and once again underlined his importance to the team.

The star's performances at the 2006 and 2010 finals were – by his own incredible standards – underwhelming, yielding just one goal, but four goals in Brazil in 2014 as Argentina reached the final has given the country renewed hope he can inspire them to a third World Cup triumph in 2018.

Another hapless defender is about to be nutmegged by the magical Lionel Messi

STATS

DOB: **24/06/87**
Country: **Argentina**
International debut: **Hungary, 17/08/05**
Caps: **123** Goals: **61**
World Cup finals appearances: **15 (2006, 2010, 2014)**
World Cup finals goals: **5**

NEYMAR

The poster boy of Brazilian football and the most expensive player in the history of the game, the Paris Saint-Germain magician is an outrageous talent who is capable of mesmerising even the meanest of defences.

The list of great Brazilian players is longer than Rio's Copacabana beach. From Pele to Ronaldo, Zico to Garrincha, the South American giants have produced some of football's most iconic names, and in Neymar the five-time world champions have unearthed yet another undisputed global superstar.

A product of the Santos academy in his home country, the forward followed a path well-travelled by his compatriots in heading to Europe when he signed for Barcelona in 2013, and in his four years in Spain the youngster helped the Catalans win two La Liga titles, the Champions League and the FIFA Club World Cup. He scored 105 times in just 186 games in the process, prompting PSG to smash the world record transfer fee by paying £200 million to take him to France in the summer of 2017.

Naturally right-footed but remarkably gifted with his left, the Brazilian can play anywhere in the forward line and is renowned for his dazzling dribbling, explosive pace and shooting ability.

He was first capped by Brazil in 2010 – while a Santos player – at the age of 18, scoring on his debut against the USA, and with three goals he was one of the stars for the Samba Boys as they secured the silver medal at the 2012 Summer Olympics in London. Four years later he captained his country at the Games in Rio, leading his team to gold this time after a memorable penalty shoot-out victory over Germany in the final.

Neymar's international goal scoring record is nothing short of phenomenal. His first hat-trick came in 2012, and when he found the back of the net in a 3-0 victory over old rivals Argentina in a World Cup qualifier in November 2016 he became only the fourth Brazilian ever to register 50 goals for his country. Only Pele, Ronaldo and Romario have scored more, but with his best and potentially most prolific years ahead of him Neymar is on course to surpass them all.

The most expensive footballer in the world, Neymar is Brazil's talisman

STATS

DOB: **05/02/92**
Country: **Brazil**
International debut: **USA, 10/08/10**
Caps: **83** Goals: **53**
World Cup finals appearances: **5 (2014)**
World Cup finals goals: **4**

MOHAMED SALAH

One of the brightest stars of African football, the gifted Egyptian winger has made an indelible mark on the European stage in recent years in the colours of Chelsea, Roma and now Liverpool.

It takes a player with a special talent to win over the Kop faithful at Anfield. Liverpool supporters have famously high standards, but from the moment Salah arrived on Merseyside in the summer of 2017 the club's devotees knew they had found someone worthy of wearing the iconic red shirt.

Salah's career began in his native Egypt with El Mokawloon in Cairo, but it was first with Basel in Switzerland and then Chelsea in the Premier League that he forged his reputation, and after three seasons in Italy with first Fiorentina and then Roma he arrived at Liverpool as one of the hottest properties in Europe. He did not disappoint, with his beguiling blend of raw pace, dribbling and natural ability to time his runs yielding 12 goals in his first 14 league appearances and confirming Liverpool's £34 million investment was money well spent.

Salah may be a hugely popular figure at Anfield but he's already a national hero in Egypt following his brilliant performances for the Pharaohs. It was his brace of goals in the pivotal qualifying match against Congo in October 2017 that ensured Egypt would be at the World Cup finals for the first time since the team qualified for Italia '90.

First capped in 2011, Salah's world-class talent was showcased on a global stage at the 2012 Olympics in London where he scored three goals as Egypt reached the quarter-finals. He subsequently top scored for Egypt with six goals in their 2014 World Cup qualifying campaign, even though they did not make it to Brazil, and he was once again his country's leading marksman at the 2017 Africa Cup of Nations in Gabon when the Pharaohs finished as runners-up.

Russia will be his first appearances in the World Cup finals but Salah has already demonstrated he deserves to be ranked right up alongside Europe and South America's finest players.

Now confirmed as one of the world's best players, Mohamed Salah is heading for stardom

STATS

DOB: **15/06/92**
Country: **Egypt**
International debut: **Sierra Leone, 03/09/11**
Caps: **56** Goals: **32**
World Cup finals appearances: **0**
World Cup finals goals: **0**

TONI KROOS

The heartbeat of midfield for both club and country, the Real Madrid and Germany star is a dazzling playmaker with the ability and vision to consistently create at the very highest level.

Arguably the most gifted of a golden generation of German players, Kroos has already won almost every domestic and international honour football has to offer but will still only be 28 and at the height of his powers when Die Mannschaft begin their defence of the World Cup in Russia.

Nicknamed 'The Professor', the midfielder is an amazingly accurate passer of the ball who selflessly creates chances for teammates – no player supplied more assists than Kroos in Brazil in 2014 as Germany were crowned world champions for a fourth time.

The playmaker began his career with Bayern Munich in 2007 and in eight seasons at the Allianz Arena he helped the German giants win three Bundesliga titles, the UEFA Champions League, the UEFA Super Cup and the FIFA Club World Cup.

In the summer of 2014 he signed a six-year deal with Real Madrid and made an immediate impact, winning the UEFA Super Cup on debut for a second time in his career after Madrid beat Sevilla in Cardiff.

Since his arrival in Spain, the midfielder has continued to add to his impressive medal haul and he was a key figure in Los Blancos' victory in the finals of the Champions League of 2016 and 2017 as well as the team's triumphs in the 2014 and 2016 FIFA Club World Cup.

Kroos first played for Germany in a friendly against Argentina in 2010 but it was his stunning form at the World Cup in Brazil in 2014 that established him as one of the game's biggest stars. Turning in a string of outstanding performances, he scored two goals in the incredible 7-1 victory over Brazil in the semi-final and after Germany had lifted the trophy – having beaten Argentina in the final – was named in the FIFA World Cup All-Star Team.

Midfield playmaker Toni Kroos has his sights set on another World Cup triumph

STATS

DOB: **04/01/90**
Country: **Germany**
International debut: **Argentina, 03/03/10**
Caps: **80** Goals: **12**
World Cup finals appearances: **11 (2010, 2014)**
World Cup finals goals: **2**

EDEN HAZARD

The jewel in the current crown of Belgium football, the Chelsea star conducts the attacking play for club and country like an orchestra and is now rated as one of the game's finest creative influences.

Watching Hazard pulling the strings from midfield provides an object lesson in vision, movement and technical control. The 27-year-old is now at the peak of his powers and there's a growing sense that with Hazard at the helm 2018 could finally be Belgium's World Cup.

His meteoric rise to the top began in France as a teenager with Lille, where he was twice named the Ligue 1 Player of the Year, but it was his move to the Premier League when he signed for Chelsea in 2012 that provided the catalyst for his transformation from promising youngster to fully fledged superstar.

He hit double figures in his first two seasons at Stamford Bridge, but the 2014/15 campaign was his most irresistible to date as he banged in 19 goals across all competitions and steered Chelsea to the title. His dazzling displays earned him the Premier League Player of the Season award as well as the Football Writers' Association Footballer of the Year accolade. He was equally destructive as the Blues were crowned champions again in 2016/17.

Hazard is already rapidly approaching the fabled 100-cap milestone for his country, having made his international debut in 2008 aged 17, and Russia will be his third appearance at a major finals. The 2014 World Cup in Brazil was sadly not the tournament debut he had dreamed of as Belgium bowed out in the quarter-finals to Argentina and the playmaker failed to score in any of his five appearances in South America.

It was a different story, however, at Euro 2016 in France. Belgium again fell in the last eight but this time Hazard shone brightly, scoring once and topping the tournament's assist charts by creating four goals for his side. Hazard continued his rich vein of form with six goals in qualifying for 2018 and is now poised to make it third time lucky in Russia.

Chelsea star Eden Hazard is usually one step ahead of the opposition

STATS

DOB: **07/01/91**
Country: **Belgium**
International debut: **Luxembourg, 19/11/08**
Caps: **82** Goals: **21**
World Cup finals appearances: **5 (2014)**
World Cup finals goals: **0**

ANTOINE GRIEZMANN

The star player at Euro 2016 and the winner of the Golden Boot, the French forward is a special player who has become one of the deadliest marksmen in the world.

A versatile player who can operate in a variety of attacking positions, Griezmann is one of the hottest properties in football and was voted La Liga's best player ahead of Lionel Messi and Cristiano Ronaldo in 2016.

The Frenchman arrived in Spain after he was spotted by scouts from Real Sociedad at a youth tournament in Paris, and the club handed him his senior debut at the age of 18 in a Copa del Rey match against Rayo Vallecano. He made 39 appearances in the 2009/10 season as Sociedad won promotion back to the top division in Spain.

Griezmann spent four more seasons in San Sebastien, scoring a total of 52 goals for the club, but in 2014 he signed a six-year deal with Atletico Madrid in a transfer reported to be worth £25 million. The left-footed forward was an instant hit at the Vicente Calderon Stadium, scoring 25 times in his first season with the club, and he was even more influential in 2015/16, finding the back of the net seven times in the competition to fire Atletico into the final of the Champions League.

After starring for the French Under-19 and Under-20 sides, Griezmann made his senior international debut against the Netherlands in 2014, but it was at the European Championships on home soil two years later that he truly made the headlines.

Greizmann was in sensational form at Euro 2016. He scored in the group stage game against Albania but it was his goals in the knockout stages – most memorably his double against Germany in the semi-final – which made him the undisputed star of the tournament. His total of six goals in France earned him the coveted Golden Boot as top scorer, as well as the European Championship Player of the Tournament award, while he later netted four times in qualifying to help his country book their place in Russia.

Top scorer at Euro 2016, will Antoine Griezmann win the Golden Boot again this summer?

STATS

DOB: **21/03/91**
Country: **France**
International debut: **Netherlands, 05/03/14**
Caps: **49** Goals: **19**
World Cup finals appearances: **5 (2014)**
World Cup finals goals: **0**

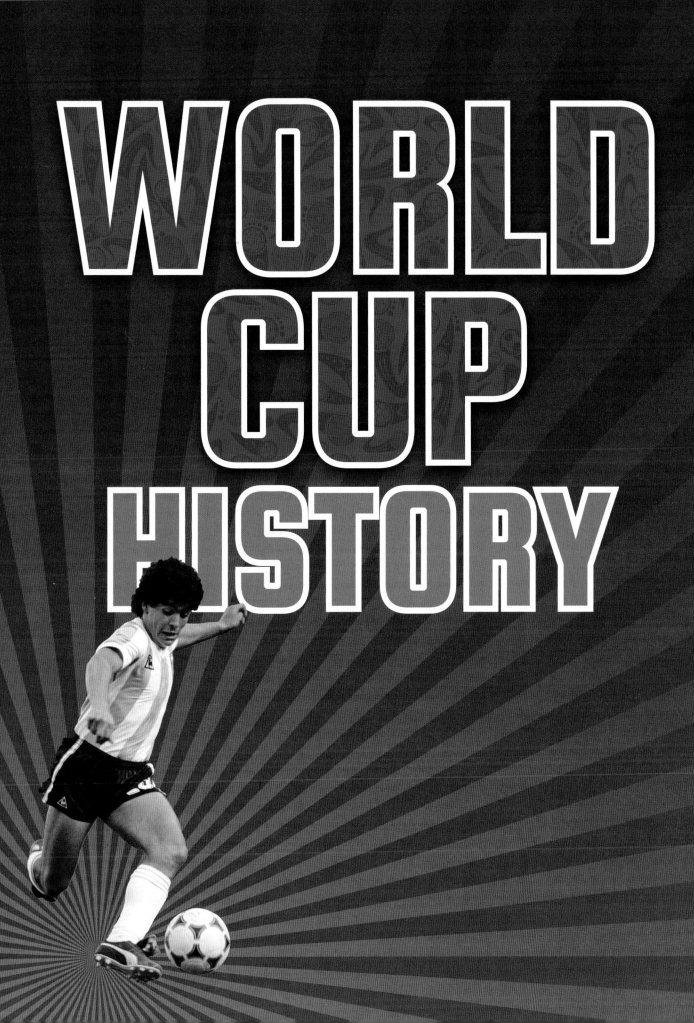

The idea of a world football championship was first raised at Fifa's inaugural meeting in Paris in 1904, but only really gained momentum in the 1920s. A proposal to hold a World Cup tournament was agreed in 1928 in Amsterdam, with Uruguay's bid to act as the host nation being accepted the following year. Since then the World Cup finals have been played 20 times, and eight nations have gone on to lift one of the two trophies (Brazil got to keep the first after winning their third tournament in 1970, although it was subsequently stolen and never seen again!).

1930, URUGUAY

Of the 13 countries who arrived in Montevideo in July 1930, only four made the three-week boat journey from Europe. Among the absentees were the four Home Nations, who had resigned from Fifa following an argument about payments to amateur players. Germany, Spain and Italy also stayed at home, leaving just France, Belgium, Romania and Yugoslavia to fly the flag for Europe.

Of that quartet only Yugoslavia won their group, after victories against Brazil and Bolivia, to reach the semi-final where they were duly crushed 6-1 by the hosts. The next day, Argentina beat the USA by the same score to join Uruguay in the final.

Although Uruguay had the advantage of playing at home, thousands of Argentinian fans made the journey across the River Plate to support their team. The recently constructed Centenary Stadium in Montevideo was packed with 93,000 fans two hours before kick-off, while behind the scenes the teams argued about which ball to use. Eventually Fifa settled the dispute by ruling that the two countries could use their preferred ball for a half each.

The original World Cup, the Jules Rimet trophy

Playing with their opponents' ball, Uruguay took an early lead, but Argentina hit back with two goals before half-time to stun the home fans into silence. The hosts, though, dominated after the break and soon equalised through inside-forward Pedro Cea. Ten minutes later left-winger Santos Iriarte restored Uruguay's lead before centre-forward Hector Castro wrapped up his side's victory in the closing seconds.

As Uruguay captain Jose Nasazzi was presented with the gold cup by Fifa President Jules Rimet, motor horns blared in the streets of Montevideo while the ships sounded their sirens in the port. Despite the disappointing turnout from Europe, the first World Cup had been a huge success.

1934, ITALY

By 1934 the World Cup was already starting to expand. No fewer than 32 countries entered the qualifying competition, with half of that number reaching the finals in Italy. For the only time in the history of the tournament the holders, Uruguay, still bitter about being snubbed by the main European powers four years earlier, declined to defend their trophy. Again, the Home Nations stayed away, the FA's dismissive attitude towards the World Cup being summed up by committee member Charles Sutcliffe, who said: "The national associations of England, Scotland, Wales and Ireland have quite enough to do in their own International Championship which seems to me a far better World Championship than the one to be staged in Rome."

This time the tournament was organised on a straight knockout basis, with the two South American representatives, Argentina and Brazil, falling at the first hurdle to Sweden and Spain respectively. Neither of the victors, though, survived the second round, leaving

The Italian team before the 1934 World Cup final

Czechoslovakia, Germany, Austria and Italy to battle it out in the semi-finals. In Milan, the hosts beat the Austrians thanks to a single goal by right-winger Enrique Guaita, one of three former Argentinian internationals in the Italian team. On the same day in Rome, Italian dictator Benito Mussolini watched Czechoslovakia defeat Germany 3-1.

The final, played in front of 45,000 fans at the Stadio Nazionale in Rome, was a tight affair. The Czechs' attractive short-passing game was eventually rewarded 20 minutes from the end when left-winger Antonin Puc scored with a long-range effort after his corner had only partially been cleared. Italy nearly fell two behind when a Czech effort hit the post, but made the most of their luck to equalise through a crazily swerving shot by left-winger Raimundo Orsi, another Argentine, with just eight minutes to play. The match moved into extra-time, centre-forward Angelo Schiavio grabbing the winner for Italy early in the first period after being set up by Guaita.

1938, FRANCE

It was, perhaps, fitting that the third World Cup was held in France in 1938 as two Frenchmen, Fifa President Jules Rimet and Henri Delaunay, Secretary of the French FA, had been instrumental in setting up the competition a decade earlier.

For a second time the tournament followed a knockout pattern, Brazil's incredible 6-5 defeat of Poland the pick of the first round matches. Two of the ties went to replays, Cuba surprisingly beating Romania and Germany going down to Switzerland despite holding a

2-0 lead at half-time. The Cubans, though, were trounced 8-0 by Sweden in the second round, while Switzerland were eliminated by Hungary, who went on to crush the Swedes 5-1 in the semi-final in Paris. In the other half of the draw, a violent encounter between Brazil and Czechoslovakia produced two broken limbs and three expulsions, and was only settled in the South Americans' favour after a replay. Brazil's World Cup, however, ended when they were beaten 2-1 in the semi-final by holders Italy, who had earlier accounted for the hosts in the second round.

The final in Paris got off to an exciting start, when both teams scored inside the first seven minutes, Pal Titkos cancelling out Gino Colaussi's opener for the Italians. Hungary, though, were finding it difficult to contain Italy's captain and playmaker Giuseppe Meazza, who provided the pass for Silvio Piola to restore the Azzurri's lead on the quarter-hour mark. Ten minutes before half-time Meazza

Giuseppe Meazza and Gyorgy Sarosi before the 1938 final

slotted the ball through to Colaussi, who beat his marker to grab his second goal. To their credit, the Hungarians refused to buckle and reduced the deficit when, following a goalmouth scramble, centre-forward Gyorgy Sarosi poked the ball home midway through the second half. Ten minutes from the end, though, Piola ensured the cup would remain in Italy with a powerful drive that whistled into the Hungarian net.

1950, BRAZIL

Appearing at their first World Cup in Brazil in 1950, England travelled to South America with high hopes that a team containing the attacking talents of Stanley Matthews, Tom Finney and Jackie Milburn would justify their tag as joint favourites alongside the hosts. Even the local press were hugely excited by England's participation, with banner headlines proclaiming 'The Kings of Football Have Arrived'.

Following a routine win over Chile in which Blackpool's Stan Mortensen headed England's first ever World Cup goal, Walter Winterbottom's team travelled from Rio de Janeiro to the mining town of Belo Horizonte to play the USA. Facing a side who had twice conceded six goals to Mexico in the qualifiers, England's stars were expected to win handsomely but after missing a host of chances and hitting the woodwork five times, they were beaten 1-0 in one of the tournament's greatest ever shocks. Another 1-0 defeat in their final match, this time against Spain, left England to

Uruguay's Schiaffino equalises against Brazil

ponder a first experience of the World Cup that had been a complete humiliation.

In a one-off experiment, the four group winners all played each other in a final pool, with the cup going to the country taking the most points. After scoring a total of 13 goals in their emphatic defeats of Sweden and Spain, this looked likely to be Brazil, especially as the hosts would only require a draw in their final match against neighbours Uruguay in the Maracana stadium to become world champions.

A Brazilian triumph seemed even more certain when right-winger Friaca gave his side the lead just two minutes after the half-time break. Uruguay, however, responded with a series of attacks and were rewarded with an equaliser from Juan Alberto Schiaffino. Ten minutes from time the massed ranks of Brazilian fans in the record 199,854 crowd were stunned for a second time when Alcides Ghiggia fired in the winner for the visitors. Brazil had no answer and, after two decades, the World Cup returned to Uruguay.

1954, SWITZERLAND

England travelled to Switzerland with their confidence at a low ebb after two shattering defeats at the hands of Hungary in the months before the World Cup. Their squad, though, was an experienced one, with an average age of 29 thanks in part to the presence of Stanley Matthews, still nipping down the wing at the age of 39.

The bizarre format of the tournament, the first to be televised, meant that the two seeded teams in each group would not play each other, only the other two supposedly weaker teams. England, then, avoided a potentially tricky fixture against Italy and instead opened their campaign against Belgium. The match was a thriller, the underdogs coming back from 3-1 down to force extra-time and, eventually, a 4-4 draw. Needing to beat the hosts to progress to the knockout stage, England won fairly comfortably thanks to goals by the Wolves duo of Jimmy Mullen and Dennis Wilshaw.

England's opponents in the quarter-finals were the holders Uruguay, who had just trounced Scotland 7-0 in their final group match. Helped by some poor goalkeeping by Birmingham's Gil Merrick, the South Americans ran out 4-2 winners

An injury to Puskas damaged Hungary's hopes in 1954

before going down by the same score to the brilliant Hungarians in the semi-finals. Their opponents in the final would be West Germany, who demolished Austria 6-1 in the other semi-final in Basel.

Having previously thrashed the Germans 8-3 in a group game, Hungary were strong favourites to triumph again in Berne and when they took a two-goal lead after just eight minutes the cup seemed destined for Budapest. Within another eight minutes, though, the Germans were level. Handicapped by an injury to their star player, inside-forward Ferenc Puskas, Hungary wilted and seven minutes from time German winger Helmut Rahn struck his second goal of the game to earn his country their first World Cup in dramatic fashion.

1958, SWEDEN

England's preparations for the World Cup in Sweden were put into disarray in February 1958 by the Munich air crash, which claimed the lives of eight Manchester United players. Among the victims were three established England internationals – the great Duncan Edwards, striker Tommy Taylor and defender Roger Byrne – who would probably have featured in Walter Winterbottom's team had they survived.

Drawn in a tough group with eventual winners Brazil, Olympic champions the Soviet Union and the formidable Austrians, England's patched-up side got off to a reasonable start with a 2-2 draw against a physical Soviet outfit. A goalless draw against the talented Brazilians gave England a good chance of progressing, but a third stalemate against an already eliminated Austria meant they would have to meet Russia again in a play-off to decide who would go through to the quarter-finals. Resisting a media campaign to start Manchester United's 20-year-old star Bobby Charlton, Winterbottom saw his team go down to a 1-0 defeat and, frustratingly, return home from the competition before both Wales and Northern Ireland.

Both those teams, though, went out in the quarter-finals to finally end British interest in

A teenage Pele plays against Wales in 1958

the tournament. Nothern Ireland were hammered 4-0 by France, while Wales were beaten by Brazil, 17-year-old striking sensation Pele grabbing the only goal. Pele then claimed a hat-trick as Brazil crushed France 5-2 in one semi-final, while hosts Sweden saw off West Germany in the other.

In the final in Stockholm, Sweden took a surprise lead after just four minutes – but there was to be no shock result. Two goals by their centre-forward Vava put Brazil ahead before half-time, and the game was pretty match settled when Pele added a magnificent third 10 minutes after the break. Brazil's left-winger Mario Zagallo made it four with 13 minutes left and, although Sweden replied with a second goal, there was still time for Pele to round off a resounding victory for the South Americans with a majestic header.

1962, CHILE

With just two defeats in their previous 17 matches, an England team featuring the likes of goal poacher Jimmy Greaves, midfield playmaker Johnny Haynes and a young Bobby Moore in their line-up went into the 1962 World Cup in Chile in fine fettle. The confident mood, though, was soon shattered by a defeat to a Hungary side who were not a patch on the 'Magical Magyars' of the 1950s.

Brazil line up in traditional pose at the 1962 finals

Written off by the press, England responded with an impressive 3-1 defeat of Argentina, Ron Flowers, Bobby Charlton and Greaves getting the goals for Walter Winterbottom's team. A dull 0-0 draw with Bulgaria then clinched England's place in the quarter-finals, where they had the misfortune to come up against the holders, Brazil.

Although missing Pele through injury, Brazil predictably proved too strong and ran out 3-1 winners, two of their goals coming from winger Garrincha, whose bandy-legged running style was the legacy of a childhood bout of polio. The other quarter-finals were won by Czechoslovakia, Yugoslavia and hosts Chile, who had earlier beaten Italy in one of the most violent games ever seen at the World Cup. Two Italian players were dismissed by the English referee Ken Aston, although the Chileans were equally to blame for some appalling scenes in a match dubbed 'The Battle of Santiago'.

The Chileans' underhand tactics were again in evidence in the semi-final, which they lost 4-2 to Brazil. Garrincha, who netted twice, was kicked throughout, and when he finally retaliated was promptly sent off. It seemed that he would miss the final against Czechoslovakia, who beat Yugoslavia 3-1 in the other semi-final, until Fifa waived his suspension following a personal plea by the Brazilian President.

As in 1958 Brazil conceded the first goal in the final, but they were soon level through Pele's replacement Amarildo. The same player set up Zito for an easy header 20 minutes from time, before Vava ensured the cup would stay in Brazil by adding a third late on.

1966, ENGLAND

Hosting the World Cup for the first time, England went into the tournament as one of the favourites, the expectation of the nation unsurprisingly intensified by manager Alf Ramsey's bold prediction that his side would win the competition.

Ramsey's confidence seemed misplaced after England opened their campaign with a disappointing 0-0 draw with Uruguay, but a trademark Bobby Charlton thunderbolt against Mexico finally got the hosts going. A 2-0 victory over the Central Americans was followed by another comfortable win against France, in a match marred by an ugly tackle by Ramsey's

Alan Ball's World Cup winners' medal from 1966

Bobby Moore shows off the World Cup at Wembley in 1966

dogged midfield enforcer, Nobby Stiles.

In the quarter-finals, England struggled to break down an uncompromising and sometimes brutal Argentina, even after the first-half dismissal of their captain, Antonio Rattin. Eventually, though, Geoff Hurst headed the winner from a cross by his West Ham team-mate Martin Peters. After the final whistle Ramsey intervened to stop his players swapping shirts with their opponents, before describing the Argentinians as 'animals' in his post-match press conference.

England's semi-final with Portugal, who had recovered from 3-0 down to beat surprise package North Korea in the previous round, was a more attractive affair. Two goals from Bobby Charlton gave the home team a healthy cushion and, although Portugal star Eusebio scored from the spot late on, England marched on to their first World Cup final.

Their opponents at Wembley were West Germany, conquerors of the Soviet Union in the other semi-final. England got off to a poor start, conceding a sloppy goal to Helmut Haller after 12 minutes. Soon, though, Hurst equalised with a header from Bobby Moore's quickly taken free-kick and then, in the second half, went ahead when Peters slammed home from close range. With the last kick of the game, however, the Germans levelled with a scrappy goal by Wolfgang Weber.

"You've beaten them once... now go out and bloody beat them again!" Ramsey told his players before the start of extra-time. And that's precisely what they did. England restored their lead when Hurst struck a fierce shot which bounced down off the crossbar, the referee ruling that the ball had crossed the line after consulting his linesman. It was Hurst, too, who confirmed his team's triumph in the closing seconds with a rasping drive into

the roof of the net, making him the first – and so far, only – player to score a hat-trick in a World Cup final.

1970, MEXICO

Often described as the best finals in the history of the competition, the 1970 tournament in Mexico provided a feast of attacking football – much of it served up by a wonderful Brazilian side featuring a host of legendary names including Pele, Rivelino and Jairzinho.

Brazil's match with holders England was the most keenly anticipated of the group stages, and lived up to expectations despite being played in blisteringly hot temperatures. England's goalkeeper Gordon Banks was in superb form, making a particularly memorable save from Pele's powerful header, but he was eventually beaten when Jairzinho rifled home what proved to be the winning goal. Victories over Romania and Czechoslovakia, though, saw England join Brazil in the quarter-finals.

In a rerun of the 1966 final, England were paired with West Germany. Alf Ramsey's team seemed set for another famous triumph when they swept into a 2-0 lead, but a mistake by goalkeeper Peter Bonetti, deputising for an unwell Banks, allowed Franz Beckenbauer to pull a goal back for the Germans. Ten minutes from time a back header from Uwe Seeler

Carlos Alberto takes the Jules Rimet trophy for keeps

looped over Bonetti to level the scores, before prolific striker Gerd Muller completed a remarkable recovery with a close-range finish in extra-time.

The Germans' luck, though, ran out in the semi-final when they went down 4-3 to Italy in an extraordinary match which featured no fewer than five goals in extra-time. In the other semi-final, Brazil made light work of their neighbours Uruguay, winning 3-1 after another glittering display.

The final in Mexico City was a dazzling spectacle, providing a fitting end to a glorious tournament. Brazil took an early lead when Pele thumped in a header, but the Italians were on level terms before the break after Roberto Boninsegna was gifted a goal by the South Americans' erratic defence. There was no stopping Brazil in the second half, however, as Gerson rattled home a long-range shot, Jairzinho scored from close range and, finally, Pele stroked a pass into the path of his captain, Carlos Alberto, who blasted in a low piledriver from the edge of the box to round off his country's third World Cup victory in magnificent style.

1974, WEST GERMANY

The 1974 tournament is primarily remembered for some scintillating performances by a Dutch team appearing at their first post-war World Cup. Led by the great Johan Cruyff and adopting a system of play dubbed 'Total Football', the Netherlands were sensational throughout.

The first round of matches, though, was most notable for the surprise elimination of Italy following a defeat by Poland, conquerors of England in the qualifiers. Another shock saw the hosts West Germany lose 1-0 to their East German neighbours, although both countries had already qualified for the second round.

For the first time, Fifa dispensed with the knockout format, instead opting for two groups of four teams from which the finalists would emerge. In the event, the last round of games provided semi-finals of sorts, the Netherlands beating a disappointing Brazil side 2-0 to top one group and West Germany defeating Poland thanks to a Gerd Muller goal on a waterlogged pitch in Frankfurt to head the other.

The final in Munich got off to an incredible start when a superb passing move by the Dutch straight from the kick-off ended with Cruyff being hacked down in the penalty area. England's sole representative at the finals, referee Jack Taylor, pointed to the spot and Johan Neeskens converted the penalty – the fastest ever goal in a World Cup final. The Netherlands continued to dominate the game but their failure to extend their lead proved costly when the Germans equalised through Paul Breitner's penalty after 27 minutes. Worse was to follow for the Dutch when Muller put his side ahead just before half-time. The Netherlands found

Johan Neeskens converts the Netherlands' penalty in the 1974 final

no way through after the break, and the tournament's outstanding team were denied the trophy their breathtaking football deserved.

1978, ARGENTINA

For a while it appeared that the 1978 tournament might not go ahead as planned in Argentina, following the imposition of a military dictatorship in the country. As worldwide protests against the generals' brutal regime gathered momentum there were demands for the finals to be played elsewhere, but Fifa refused to change the venue.

Whatever their political views, the Argentinian public supported their team with a passion rarely seen at previous tournaments, showering their heroes with ticker tape whenever they made their entrance. Despite losing their final group match to Italy, conquerors of England in the qualifiers, the home side easily progressed into the second round, which again was split into two pools of four. After picking up a win and a draw in their first two matches, the Argentinians needed to beat Peru by four goals in their last game to pip Brazil for a place in the final. To nobody's surprise, the Peruvians simply folded and were thrashed 6-0, strike partners Mario Kempes and Leopoldo Luque grabbing two goals each. Conspiracy theorists had a field day, suggesting that the Peruvians

had either been bribed or that their goalkeeper, the Argentinian-born Ramon Quiroga, had given the hosts a helping hand.

Mario Kempes scores in the World Cup final in 1978

The other final group was made up of four European teams: Austria, the Netherlands, Italy and West Germany. The key match was between the Netherlands and Italy, which the Dutch only needed to draw to reach the final. In the event, they won the game 2-1 despite trailing at half-time.

Roared on by a near-hysterical crowd in Buenos Aires, Argentina took the lead in the final through the prolific Kempes. A late equaliser by the Dutch sent the match into extra-time, but the hosts were not to be denied. Inspired by the midfield promptings of little Ossie Ardiles, they added further goals through Kempes and winger Daniel Bertoni to become world champions for the first time.

1982, SPAIN

After missing out on the two previous tournaments, England qualified for the first 24-team World Cup in unconvincing style. Once there, however, Ron Greenwood's team got off to a perfect start in their opening game against France when midfielder Bryan Robson drilled home after just 27 seconds – still the one

Trevor Francis helps outwit France in 1982

Poland thanks to two goals by the tournament's top scorer, Paolo Rossi. Later that evening, an enthralling match between West Germany and France ended in a 3-3 draw after the French had led 3-1 in extra-time. For the first time ever at the World Cup a penalty shoot-out finally settled the outcome, the Germans emerging as the winners.

The first half of the final in Madrid was a tense affair, the best chance falling to the Italians when they were awarded a penalty. Left-back Antonio Cabrini, though, wasted the opportunity, sending his kick wide. In the end it mattered little, as Italy dominated after the break and scored three times through Rossi, Marco Tardelli and Alessandro Altobelli. Paul Breitner replied for the Germans, but far too late to prevent Italy claiming their third World Cup.

1986, MEXICO

Initially awarded to Colombia, the venue for the 1986 tournament was later switched for economic reasons to Mexico, who became the first nation to host the competition twice.

After a stress-free qualifying campaign, England were expected to do well but they got off to a dreadful start, losing their opening match to Portugal and then being held by Morocco. Adding to manager Bobby Robson's woes, he also lost two of his key players, injured skipper Bryan Robson and midfielder Ray Wilkins, suspended after becoming the first England player to be sent off at the finals.

of the fastest goals in the competition's history. England went on to win the match 3-1, and after straightforward victories over Czechoslovakia and Kuwait, topped their group with something to spare.

A tough draw in the second stage saw England paired with old adversaries West Germany and hosts Spain. After a 0-0 draw with the Germans, England needed to beat the Spanish by two goals to reach the semi-finals but were held to another goalless draw. Frustratingly, two excellent chances were spurned by substitutes Kevin Keegan and Trevor Brooking, both making their first appearances of the finals after missing the earlier part of the tournament through injury.

In the first semi-final Italy, who had earlier sneaked through their first round group with three draws, beat

However, the new-look team Robson fielded in

Maradona's 'Hand of God' goal against England

the must-win final group game against Poland performed much better, striker Gary Lineker scoring all three goals in a convincing 3-0 win. Another excellent display, and two more Lineker goals, saw off Paraguay in the last 16, setting up a quarter-final with Argentina.

The match in Mexico City hinged on two moments involving Diego Maradona, Argentina's captain and star player. Shortly after the break he flicked the ball into the net with his hand but, despite furious protests from England's players, the goal stood. Minutes later, Maradona dribbled past the entire England defence before planting the ball past goalkeeper Peter Shilton. Golden Boot winner Lineker replied with a late header, but it was not enough to save England.

Maradona scored another magical goal as Argentina breezed past Belgium and into the final. Their opponents were West Germany, conquerors of France in the other semi-final. The South Americans took a two-goal lead and appeared to be heading for a comfortable victory until the Germans scored twice in the final quarter hour, both goals coming from corners. There was still enough time left, though, for the brilliant Maradona to settle the game in Argentina's favour, his superb defence-splitting pass setting up midfielder Jorge Burruchaga for the winner.

1990, ITALY

The 1990 tournament in Italy provided some memorable moments but overall was a rather disappointing spectacle, plagued by overly cautious football which resulted in the lowest goals-per-game average of any World Cup.

From an England perspective, though, the finals were the most exciting since Bobby Moore and co. triumphed in 1966. Nevertheless, Italia '90 started poorly for Bobby Robson's men with a draw against Ireland. Another draw, against a powerful Netherlands side, was more encouraging, midfielder Paul Gascoigne earning rave reviews for a dynamic performance. Qualification was then achieved with a scrappy win over plucky minnows Egypt, defender Mark Wright scoring the only goal.

Under pressure from his senior players, Robson had switched to a sweeper system and he retained the formation for the last 16 meeting with Belgium. A tense game looked to be heading for penalties until Gascoigne's free-kick was superbly volleyed in by David Platt for the winner. 'Gazza', as he was now known to

everybody, was again outstanding in a nerve-wracking quarter-final against surprise package Cameroon, which England won 3-2 in extra-time, with Gary Lineker firing in the second of two penalties to settle the match.

In the semi-final against West Germany in Turin England fell behind to a cruelly deflected free-kick, but hit back to equalise through Lineker. Extra-time brought no further goals, just a booking for a tearful Gazza – which meant he would miss the final should England get there. However, to the dismay of 30 million fans watching back home, both Stuart Pearce and Chris Waddle missed in the penalty shoot-out and the Germans went through.

Their opponents in Rome, Argentina, came through a semi-final shoot-out of their own, against Italy. An ugly, bad-tempered final, which saw two Argentinians dismissed, was also decided from the spot, West Germany's Andreas Brehme firing home late on to give his country a third world title.

Gazza before those famous tears in the semi-final against Germany

1994, USA

For the first time in the history of the World Cup the 1994 tournament was held in a nation, the USA, where football is only a minor sport. Nevertheless, the American public responded enthusiastically, with the total attendance of 3.6 million being the highest ever at the finals so far.

The World Cup came to Chicago in 1994

The fans were rewarded with some exciting games in the opening round, and a number of shock results. Bulgaria beat Argentina, Saudi Arabia defeated Belgium while Jack Charlton's Ireland got the better of a highly fancied Italy. All those teams went through to the second round, however, although Argentina did so without their captain Diego Maradona, who was sensationally banned from the rest of the tournament after failing a drugs test.

The South Americans were soon eliminated, losing a five-goal thriller to Romania in the last 16. Another east European team, Bulgaria, pulled off an even bigger surprise in the quarter-final when they came from behind to beat Germany. The Bulgarians' opponents in the semi-final were Italy, with Brazil and Sweden completing the final four. Both games were close, but neither of the underdogs survived: in Pasadena, the Swedes were undone by a late goal by Romario, while in New York, the Bulgarians succumbed to Italy's pony-tailed talisman Roberto Baggio, who claimed both goals in his side's 2-1 win.

In a repeat of the 1970 final, Italy and Brazil met to decide the destination of the trophy in Los Angeles. Despite the array of attacking talent on show, the game never really got going and it was no surprise that the tie had to be settled by penalties. Italy missed two and Brazil one before Baggio, the undoubted star of the tournament, blazed his kick high over the bar to gift the South Americans their fourth World Cup.

1998, FRANCE

The World Cup was revamped for the 1998 tournament in France, the most important innovations seeing the number of entrants expanding from 24 to 32 and the introduction of the 'golden goal' to settle knockout matches which went into extra-time.

Having missed out on the finals altogether four years earlier, England were determined to build on their good showing at Euro '96. Glenn Hoddle's side began with a comfortable victory over Tunisia in Marseille but then lost to Romania, falling to a last-minute winner by Dan Petrescu after 18-year-old striker Michael Owen had come off the bench to level the scores. Needing to beat Colombia to advance, Darren Anderton and the outstanding David Beckham came up with the goals to keep England in the tournament.

In the last 16 meeting with Argentina in St Etienne both sides netted from the spot in the early stages, before Owen put England ahead with a brilliant

Zinedine Zidane after scoring in the 1998 final

Brazil's preparations for the final in Paris were thrown into turmoil when star striker Ronaldo suffered a convulsive fit shortly before kick-off. Although he played, Ronaldo understandably looked a shadow of his normal self and France won the match convincingly, two headers by their playmaker Zinedine Zidane settling the outcome before Emmanuel Petit added an extra gloss to the hosts' victory with a third goal in injury-time.

2002, JAPAN AND SOUTH KOREA

The first World Cup to be held in Asia, the 2002 tournament in Japan and South Korea was attended by hordes of friendly supporters from the host nations. The local fans were repaid with consistently excellent displays by their own countries, who were among a number of less fancied teams to spring major surprises.

individual goal. However, the South Americans levelled the scores before half-time and then took the initiative when Beckham was sent off for a petulant kick at Diego Simeone who had fouled him. A man short, England hung on bravely through extra-time but lost out on penalties after misses by Paul Ince and David Batty.

Argentina's World Cup ended in the next round when they lost to the Netherlands, who in turn went out in a semi-final shoot-out to Brazil. The South Americans' opponents in the final were France, who came through their semi-final against surprise outfit Croatia thanks to two goals by defender Lilian Thuram.

The main shock in the group stage was the elimination of holders France after defeats by Senegal and Denmark. Portugal, too, fell by the wayside following a 1-0 loss to South Korea. There was an upset, too, in England's group where Argentina failed to qualify, the key result being the South Americans' 1-0 defeat to Sven-Goran Eriksson's men, England skipper David Beckham scoring from the penalty spot. The Three Lions had little difficulty in disposing of Denmark 3-0 in the last 16, thanks to Michael Owen, Emile Heskey, and an own goal.

In the quarter-final against Brazil, Owen gave his side the lead

David Beckham converts a penalty against Argentina

before Rivaldo equalised on the stroke of half-time. In the second half Ronaldinho floated a free-kick over David Seaman's head from fully 40 yards before being sent off. England, though, failed to make the extra man count and slipped out of the competition.

Both the semi-finals were decided by a single goal: Brazil accounting for Turkey and Germany finally seeing off South Korea, who had knocked out Italy and Spain in the previous rounds. In the first ever World Cup meeting between two titans of the tournament, Ronaldo proved to be the difference between the teams, grabbing both goals as Brazil won 2-0 to claim a fifth World Cup title.

2006, GERMANY

An unwritten rule of the World Cup states that the winners virtually always come from the continent where the tournament is played. The 2006 finals in Germany took that rule a step further with all four semi-finalists hailing from Europe.

Among the European sides of whom great things were expected were Sven-Goran Eriksson's England. Drawn in an easy-looking group and with a squad of players dubbed 'the golden generation', the Three Lions made painfully hard work of their opening fixtures, beating Paraguay by a single goal and taking more than 80 minutes to break the deadlock against Trinidad and Tobago before running out 2-0 winners. England then played much better against Sweden, but were held to a draw after the Scandinavians cancelled out a superb volley from Joe Cole and a Steven Gerrard header.

In the last 16, England were unconvincing once more against Ecuador, surviving a number of scares before skipper David Beckham's free-kick proved decisive. With Michael Owen sidelined by injury, Eriksson adopted a cautious strategy against Portugal in the quarter-final, employing Wayne Rooney as a lone striker. The game turned out to be a cagey affair, the key moment coming when Rooney was sent off for stamping on Ricardo Carvalho. England hung on grimly through extra-time before the match was settled by penalties. The old shoot-out hoodoo struck again as Frank Lampard, Gerrard and Jamie Carragher all missed.

The Portuguese, though, were not so fortunate in the semi-final against France, going out to a Zinedine Zidane spot-kick. The other semi-final between Italy and Germany was set to go to penalties until the hosts were undone by two goals at the end of extra-time.

The final in Berlin got off to a spectacular start when France were awarded a controversial penalty after just

Wayne Rooney sees red in the 2006 quarter-final

seven minutes. Zidane, cool as ever, chipped his shot in off the crossbar, but Italy levelled soon afterwards through Marco Materazzi's firm header. Both sides missed chances to win the match before Zidane was sent off in extra-time for head-butting Materazzi in the chest. Italy failed to take advantage of their numerical superiority and, as in 1994, the final was decided by the lottery of penalties. The fall guy on this occasion was France's David Trezeguet, whose miss allowed Fabio Grosso the chance to clinch the trophy. Showing no sign of nerves, the left-back swept the ball high into the corner of the net and Italy were world champions for a fourth time.

2010, SOUTH AFRICA

The first World Cup to be played in Africa generated huge anticipation and support across the continent and, for England, the familiar feeling of expectation after an impressive qualifying campaign. The Three Lions may have had a new manager in Fabio Capello, but it was the same old story as the fading embers of the golden generation flattered to deceive.

A draw with the USA best remembered for a howler by goalkeeper Rob Green and a forgettable goalless stalemate against Algeria meant England needed to beat Slovenia to advance to the last 16, which they did thanks to Jermain Defoe's strike. That was as far as they would go, though, as a rampant Germany put them to the sword. England were left to rue what might have been when Frank Lampard's shot clearly bounced over the line but was not awarded as a goal. That would have made the score 2-2 yet, from there, they capitulated to a 4-1 defeat.

Germany put four more past an Argentina side managed by Diego Maradona to advance to the semi-finals where they were edged out 1-0 by Spain, a repeat of the scoreline from the Euro 2008 final. It was the third 1-0 win for the miserly Spanish, and their fifth clean sheet of the tournament.

Two other leading European nations did not even reach the knockout phase. Defending champions Italy finished bottom of their group, drawing with Paraguay and New Zealand, then losing to Slovakia. Their opponents in the 2006 final, France, departed alongside South Africa from a group topped by Uruguay.

The host nation's elimination meant the whole continent threw their support behind Ghana, the one African country to qualify for the last 16. They had reason to cheer when Asamoah Gyan scored the

Andres Iniesta celebrates his winning goal in the 2010 final

winner in extra-time against the USA, but the striker could not repeat his match-winning heroics in the quarter-final, missing a penalty with the very last kick of the game. He was not the main villain of the piece, however: that role fell to Uruguay's Luis Suarez who, in the incident that led to the penalty, deliberately handled the ball on the line to prevent a Ghanaian goal. With the match ending 1-1, Uruguay won the ensuing shoot-out, sending all of Africa into mourning.

The South Americans' opponents in the semi-final were the Netherlands, who had stunned Brazil in the last eight, a Wesley Sneijder brace overturning a one-goal deficit. And Sneijder was on target once again as the Dutch ended Uruguay's hopes with a 3-2 win in the last four.

That result meant there would be a new name on the trophy in the decider in Johannesburg. The final, refereed by Howard Webb, was a hot-headed encounter, with the Englishman booking 13 players including the dismissal of Dutchman Johnny Heitinga for two yellow cards. With the Spanish defence proving impregnable once again, Andres Iniesta settled the tie with the only goal deep into extra-time. Another 1-0 win for Spain, the eighth winners of the World Cup.

2014, BRAZIL

The build up to the 2014 finals in Brazil was overshadowed by large and angry street demonstrations against the cost of staging the tournament in a country suffering from various

Mario Gotze (left) is ecstatic after scoring the winner in the 2014 final

Giorgio Chiellini during his side's 1-0 win and was subsequently punished with a nine-match ban from international football.

The first knockout round threw up some fascinating fixtures and five extremely close encounters. In a near-hysterical atmosphere in Belo Horizonte, Brazil just sneaked through against Chile on penalties, while plucky Costa Rica saw off Greece in the same manner despite playing with just 10 men for nearly an hour. Three other matches also went to extra-time, Argentina, Belgium and Germany eventually getting the better of Switzerland, the USA and Algeria respectively.

In the most exciting of the four quarter-finals Brazil overcame Colombia, despite a sixth goal of the tournament for Golden Boot winner James Rodriguez. In the other games, Germany beat France 1-0, Argentina defeated Belgium by the same score, and the Netherlands won a shoot-out with Costa Rica after bringing penalty-saving specialist goalkeeper Tim Krul off the bench.

The first semi-final in Belo Horizonte between Brazil and Germany was an extraordinary affair, the hosts' makeshift defence collapsing into a complete shambles as they were torn apart time and again by swift counter-attacks. After half an hour the rampant Germans led 5-0, before eventually winning 7-1 in the biggest ever hammering of a home nation at the finals. The second semi-final was more cagey, Argentina finally beating the Netherlands on penalties after a 0-0 draw.

The final in Rio de Janeiro, too, was predictably tense. Argentina looked to their talisman Lionel Messi for inspiration but he was largely held in check by a well-organised German outfit. Eventually Germany managed to break the deadlock deep into extra-time when substitute Mario Gotze volleyed home – the last, and the most significant, of a joint-record 171 goals at the tournament.

economic woes and bedevilled by government corruption. However, once the tournament kicked off the football-obsessed Brazilian people became engrossed by their heroes' attempts to lift the trophy for a sixth time.

In the opening match, the hosts got off to a flying start, coming from a goal down to beat Croatia 3-1 in Sao Paulo. Backed by thousands of noisy, passionate samba-swaying fans in the stadium and tens of millions in the wider country, Brazil would clearly take some stopping and their passage to the knockout stage was secured with an emphatic 4-1 victory against Cameroon, with star striker Neymar scoring twice.

Elsewhere in the group stages, the big story was the unexpected demise of reigning champions Spain, who were crushed 5-1 by the Netherlands in their first match and then lost 2-0 to Chile to become the first country to be eliminated. In the so-called 'Group of Death', meanwhile, an England side led by veteran coach Roy Hodgson and made up of mix of old stagers and promising younger players lost narrowly to both Italy and Uruguay, making their final fixture against surprise group winners Costa Rica a dead rubber. In the event, a much-changed England team managed a 0-0 draw so went home having failed to win a match at the finals for the first time since 1958. There was rather more drama in the other fixture in the group, where feisty Uruguayan striker Luis Suarez bit Italian defender

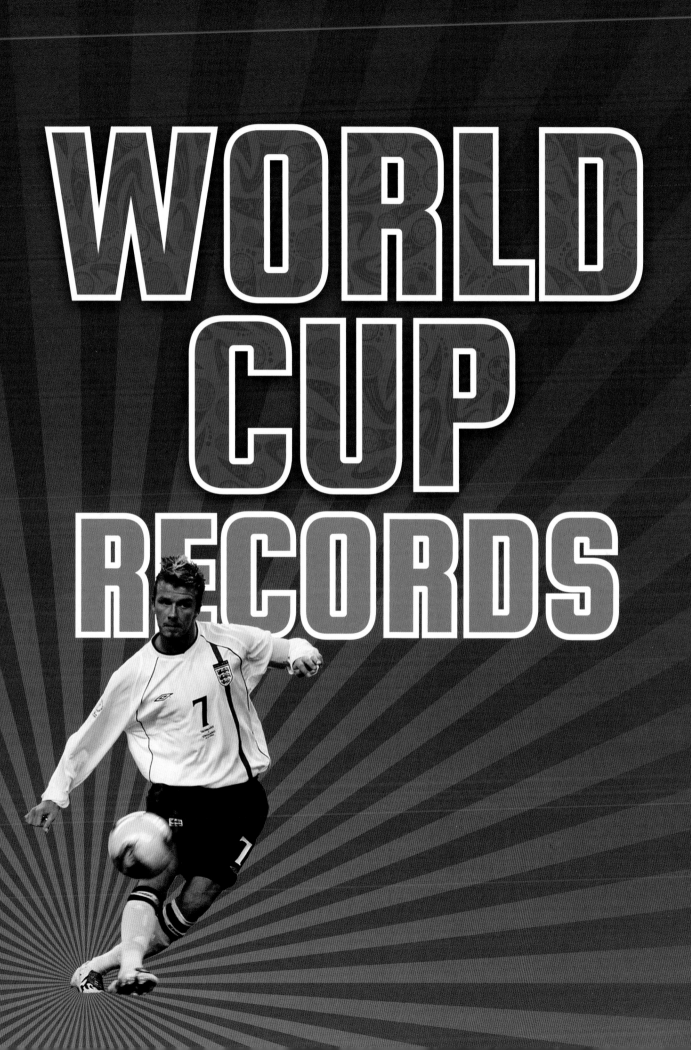

WORLD CUP RECORDS

Pele (top) leads the celebrations during Brazil's 1970 World Cup victory

TEAM RECORDS

• The most successful country in the history of the World Cup are Brazil, who have won the competition a record five times in all – in 1958, 1962, 1970, 1994 and 2002.

• **Italy and current holders Germany are Europe's leading nations with four wins each. South American neighbours Argentina and Uruguay have both won the competition twice, the Uruguayans emerging victorious when the pair met in the first ever World Cup final in Montevideo in 1930. The only other countries to claim the trophy are England (1966), France (1998) and Spain (2010).**

• Including both Japan and South Korea – who were joint hosts for the 2002 edition – and counting 2018 hosts Russia, the World Cup has been staged in 17 different countries.

• **The first nation to stage the tournament twice were Mexico (in 1970 and 1986), while Italy (1934 and 1990), France (1938 and 1998), Germany (1974 and 2006) and Brazil (1950 and 2014) have also played the role of hosts on two occasions.**

• Brazil are the only country to have played at all 20 tournaments, and will stretch their record to 21 in 2018. Germany have played in a record eight finals, have played in the most games (106), scored the most goals in total (224) and conceded the most (121).

• **Hungary hold the record for the most goals scored in a single tournament, banging in 27 in just five games at the 1954 finals in Switzerland. Even this impressive tally, though, was not quite enough for the 'Magical Magyars' to lift the trophy as they lost 3-2 in the final against West Germany, a team they had annihilated 8-3 earlier in the tournament.**

• Hungary also hold the record for the biggest ever victory at the finals, demolishing El Salvador 10-1 at the 1982 tournament in Spain. That, though, was a reasonably close encounter compared to the biggest win in qualifying, Australia's 31-0 massacre of American Samoa in 2001, a game in which Aussie striker Archie Thompson smashed in a record 13 goals.

• **If Germany manage to win the trophy again in Russia they will become only the third nation to retain the trophy after Italy (in 1938) and Brazil (in 1962). Meanwhile, the Netherlands are the only country to have played in three finals – in 1974, 1978 and 2010 – and lost them all.**

INDIVIDUAL RECORDS

• The legendary Pele is the only player in World Cup history to have been presented with three winners' medals. The Brazilian striker enjoyed his first success as a 17-year-old in 1958 when he scored twice in a 5-2 rout of hosts Sweden in the final, and was a winner again four years later in Chile despite hobbling out of the tournament with a torn leg muscle in the second match. He then made it a hat-trick in 1970, setting a brilliant Brazil side on the road to a convincing 4-1 victory against Italy in the final with a superb header.

• **Fellow Brazilian Cafu is the only player to have appeared in three finals, in 1994, 1998 and 2002, winning two and losing one.**

• The leading overall scorer in the World Cup is Germany striker Miroslav Klose, who notched 16 goals in total at four tournaments between 2002 and 2014.

Geoff Hurst – the only man to score a hat-trick in the World Cup final – slams the ball home against West Germany

The individual tournament scoring record is held by French striker Just Fontaine, who scored 13 goals at the 1958 finals in Sweden.

• **England's Geoff Hurst is the only player to score a hat-trick in a World Cup final, finding the net three times against West Germany at Wembley in 1966. His second goal, which gave England a decisive 3-2 lead in extra-time, was the most controversial in World Cup history and German fans still maintain that his shot bounced on the line after striking the crossbar rather than over it. Naturally, England fans tend to agree with the eagle-eyed Russian linesman who awarded the goal.**

• Just two players have appeared at a record five World Cups: German midfield general Lothar Matthaus (1982-98) and Mexican goalkeeper Antonio Carbajal (1950-66). Italy goalkeeper Gianluigi Buffon was also selected for five World Cup squads (1998-2014) but failed to make an appearance at the first of those tournaments.

• **The youngest player to appear at the finals is Norman Whiteside, who was just 17 and 41 days when he made his World Cup debut for Northern Ireland against Yugoslavia at the 1982 tournament in Spain. The competition's oldest player, meanwhile,** is Colombia goalkeeper Faryd Mondragon, who was aged 43 and three days when he played against Japan at the 2014 tournament in Brazil.

• England's Peter Shilton (1982-90) and France's Fabien Barthez (1998-2006) jointly hold the record for most clean sheets at the finals, with 10 each. Italy's Walter Zenga, though, holds the record for the most consecutive clean sheets, keeping the ball out of his net for 517 minutes at the 1990 tournament.

• **The fastest goal in World Cup history was scored by Hakan Sukur, who struck for Turkey after just 11 seconds in the third place play-off against hosts South Korea in 2002. Hungary's Laszlo Kiss scored the fastest hat-trick, finding the net three times in eight minutes after coming on as a sub against El Salvador in 1982.**

MISCELLANEOUS RECORDS

• Living up to their reputation for ruthless efficiency, Germany are the most successful side in World Cup shoot-outs, winning all four of their penalty duels including one in 1990 when they beat England in the semi-finals before going on to lift the trophy after a scrappy 1-0 victory over Argentina in the final. Argentina have taken part in a record five shoot-outs, also winning four.

Germany's Tim Borowski slots home during the 2006 penalty shoot-out against Argentina

• As most England fans know, the Three Lions have a dreadful record in World Cup shoot-outs, losing all three they have been involved in: against Germany in 1990, Argentina in 1998, and Portugal in 2006. The only other country to lose three shoot-outs are Italy, although they finally managed to win one when they defeated France on penalties in the 2006 final.

• The most unfortunate country in World Cup history are Scotland, who have made eight appearances at the finals without once advancing to the knockout stages. The Scots, though, were desperately unfortunate to be eliminated on goal difference in 1974, 1978 and 1982. Mexico, meanwhile, have appeared at a record 15 finals without once advancing beyond the quarter-final stage.

• Argentina and Germany have met a record seven times at the finals (as have Brazil and Sweden), including in a record three finals (in 1986, 1990 and most recently in 2014).

• A record 171 goals were scored in total at both the 1998 and 2014 finals.

• Russia's Oleg Salenko scored a record five goals in his side's 6-1 hammering of Cameroon in 1994. In the same match Roger Milla became the oldest player ever to score at the finals when he grabbed the Africans' consolation goal aged 42 and 39 days.

• A total of 169 players have been sent off at the finals. Brazil lead the way with 11 dismissals.

• The only player to score for both teams in a World Cup match is the Netherlands' Ernie Brandts, who found the net at both ends against Italy in 1978.

• Discounting goals scored in shoot-outs, three players have notched a record four penalties at the World Cup: Portugal's Eusebio in 1966, the Netherlands' Rob Rensenbrink in 1978 and Gabriel Batistuta with two for Argentina at both the 1994 and 1998 tournaments.

• The highest scoring match at the finals saw Austria beat hosts Switzerland 7-5 in 1954. The Austrians recovered from 3-0 down to win the match, a feat matched by Portugal when they beat North Korea 5-3 in the quarter-final at Goodison Park in 1966.

• The record attendance for a World Cup match is 199,854 at the 1950 final between Brazil and Uruguay at the Maracana Stadium in Rio de Janeiro. The lowest attendance stands at just 300 for the 1930 clash between Peru and Romania in Montevideo.

• **Brazilian coach Carlos Alberto Parreira managed five different countries at a record six finals: Kuwait (1982), United Arab Emirates (1990), Brazil (1994 and 2006), Saudi Arabia (1998), and South Africa (2010). Much-travelled Yugoslav Bora Milutinovic also coached five countries at the World Cup finals, starting out with Mexico in 1986 and then moving on to Costa Rica (1990), USA (1994), Nigeria (1998) and China (2002).**

• The only coach to win the trophy twice is Vittorio Pozzo, with Italy in 1934 and 1938. Just two men have won the competition as both a player and a coach: Brazil's Mario Zagallo (in 1958, 1962 and 1970) and Germany's Franz Beckenbauer (in 1974 and 1990).

• **Ravshan Irmatov from Uzbekistan refereed a record nine matches at the World Cup at the 2010 and 2014 finals.**

ENGLAND RECORDS

• Goalkeeper Peter Shilton holds the record for the most England appearances at the World Cup finals, playing in 17 matches between 1982 and 1990. Shilton is also the oldest England player to feature at the tournament, making his last appearance aged 40 and 295 days against hosts Italy in the play-off for third place in 1990.

• **With 10 goals to his name, Gary Lineker is England's record scorer at the World Cup. Lineker struck six times at the 1986 tournament – itself a record by an England player – to win the Golden Boot, and then added four more goals at Italia '90 to help his country reach the semi-finals. Along with Geoff Hurst, Lineker is also one of just two England players to score a hat-trick at the finals, grabbing all three of his team's goals in a 3-0 win against Poland in 1986.**

• The only England player to be selected for four World Cups is Bobby Charlton, although he failed to make an appearance at his first tournament in Sweden in 1958.

Gary Lineker is England's all-time leading goalscorer at the World Cup

David Beckham is the only England player to have scored at three finals, netting against Colombia (1998), Argentina (2002) and Ecuador (2006).

• **England scored a record 11 goals at the 1966 finals, and also enjoyed a record streak of five consecutive wins at the tournament on their way to lifting the Jules Rimet trophy. A sixth consecutive win followed with victory over Romania in England's first match of the 1970 finals in Mexico.**

A teenaged Michael Owen made a huge impact at the 1998 World Cup

• Manchester United midfielder Bryan Robson scored the fastest ever England goal at a World Cup – and the fourth fastest in World Cup history – when he struck after just 27 seconds against France in 1982. England went on to win the match 3-1.

• The youngest England player to appear at the World Cup is Michael Owen, who was aged 18 and 183 days when he came on as a sub against Tunisia in 1998. Seven days later Owen became England's youngest ever scorer at the finals when he fired home in a 2-1 defeat against Romania.

• England used a record 21 players at the 2014 tournament. At the other end of the scale, in an era when substitutes were not permitted, England used just 12 players at the 1962 finals.

• Three players have captained England at a record 10 World Cup matches: Billy Wright (1950-58), **Bobby Moore (1966-70) and David Beckham (2002-06).**

• Just three England players have been sent off at the World Cup: Ray Wilkins (for throwing the ball at the referee against Morocco in 1986); David Beckham (for retaliating after being fouled against Argentina in 1998); and Wayne Rooney (for stamping on an opponent against Portugal in 2006).

• The last player to make his debut for England at the finals was Leeds' Allan Clarke, who scored from the penalty spot in a 1-0 win against Czechoslovakia in 1970.

• England have only lost consecutive games at the same finals on two occasions, in 1950 when they were beaten 1-0 by both the USA and Spain, and in 2014 when they frustratingly went down 2-1 against both Italy and Uruguay.